War at Sea

1939-1945

On 25 August 1939 the German battleship *Schleswig-Holstein* entered the harbour of Danzig, at that time a Free City. The inhabitants welcomed this friendly visit, and had no idea that it was set to start the Second World War. German soldiers were concealed below the ship's deck, and during the night of 1 September they left the ship to capture the Polish Westerplatte, which had been bombarded by the *Schleswig-Holstein*'s guns (see page 15).

War at Sea
1939-1945

Jürgen Rohwer

CAXTON EDITIONS

© Urbes Verlag Hans Jürgen Hansen 1992
English translation © Chatham Publishing 1996

First published in Great Britain in 1996 by
Chatham Publishing, an imprint of
Gerald Duckworth & Co Ltd

First published in Germany in 1992 under the title
Der Krieg zur see 1939-1945 by
Urbes Verlag Hans Jürgen Hansen
D-8542291 Gräfelfing vor Munchen

British Library Cataloguing in Publication Data
A catalogue record for this book is available from
the British Library

This edition published 2001 by Caxton Edition,
an imprint of The Caxton Publishing Group
ISBN 1 84067 3621

Idea, conception and editing by Clas Broder Hansen
Research and selection of photographs by Clas Broder Hansen,
Hans Jürgen Hansen and Prof Dr Jürgen Rohwer

Translated by Keith Thomas
Typeset by Fathom Graphics, Exeter
Printed and bound by C.T.P.S.

Contents

Acknowledgements

For their valued assistance in completing this work, and in particular for their aid in procuring and verifying illustrations, the author and publisher are indebted to Dr Dean Allard, Director of the Centre of Naval History in Washington, Captain 1st class Ranga Igor Amosov of the Voenno Istoricheskiy Institut in Moscow, Jim Andow of the Hulton Deutch Collection in London, Horst Bredow of the Traditionsarchiv Unterseeboote in Cuxhaven-Altenbruch, Martina Caspers of the Koblenz Bundesarchiv, Alice S Creighton of the US Naval Academy, Nimitz Library of Annapolis, Margit Fieguth of Senden, C R Haberlein of the Washington Center of Naval History, Prof Dr Kenneth Hagan of the US Naval Academy, Nimitz Library, in Annapolis, Elaine Hart of the London Picture Library, The Illustrated London News, Meinhart Janssen of the *Prinz Eugen* Kameradschaft of Schortens, Rear Admiral Jean Kessler of the Service Historique de la Marine at Vincennes, Captain (ret) Kurt Kroeger of Wilhelmshaven, Jennifer Lee of the Annapolis Naval Institute Press, Patty Maddocks of the US Naval Institute, Photo Library, in Annapolis, Philippe Masson of the Service Historique de la Marine at Vincennes, Helga Müller of the Bildarchiv J K Piekalkewicz of Rösrath-Hoffnungsthal, Otto H Nachtigall of Dortmund, Flotilla Admiral Niemann of the Mürwick Navy School at Flensburg, Prof Dr Tadeusz Panecki of the Warsaw Woyskowy Institut Historyezny, David Perry of the London Imperial War Museum, Mrs Pfeffer of the Koblenz Bundesarchiv, Dr Robert Scheina, Senior Historian of the US Coast Guard in Washington, Eberhard Schmidt of the Mürwick Navy School historical armaments training centre at Flensburg, Jürgen Schneider of Watermill Films in Munich, Dr Cornelis Schulten, Director of the Amsterdam Rijksinstitut voor Oorlogsdocumentatie, Rear Admiral Renato Sicurezza, Head of the historical office of the navy in Rome, Dr Peter Simkins of the Imperial War Museum in London, Brig Gen (USMC, ret) Edwin Simmons, Director of the Historical Center and Museum of the US Marine Corps in Washington, Regina Strother of the Historical Center of the US Marine Corps in Washington, Jim Sutton of the Naval Institute Press of Annapolis, Peter Tamm of Hamburg, Rear Admiral (ret.) Prof. Dr Saburo Toyama of Yokohama, Dr Trumpf of the Koblenz Bundesarchiv, HA Vadnais Jr, Head Curator of the Washington Naval Historical Center, Mr Williams of the London Imperial War Museum and Dr Robert Wolfe of the US National Archives in Washington.

The following supplied original illustrations: the Janusz Piekalkiewicz picture archive, the picture service of the Süddeutsche Zeitung, the Koblenz Federal Archive, ECPA photo cinema video des armées, the Fototeca US in Rome, the Historical Collection of the Mürwick Navy School, the Illustrated London News, the Imperial War Museum, Captain (ret) Kurt Kroeger, the Musée de la Marine, National Archives Photographic Services, the National Archives Trust Fund, the Nimitz Library of the US Naval Academy, the Peter Tamm collection, Skzuo Fukui Tokyo, the Ullstein picture service, the US Coast Guard, the Photo Archives of the US Naval Institute, the U-boat Tradition Archive, the WZ picture service and the naval archive of the Stuttgart Library of Contemporary History and the archive of the Urbes publishing house.

Foreword

During a conversation between the publisher and myself, which took place in the Stuttgart Library of Contemporary History, we discussed the possibility of a joint publication based on the comprehensive marine photographic archive held by the library. Our discussion centred on the production of a new, liberally illustrated history of the naval aspects of the Second World War, and eventually we drew up a plan. The project looked promising owing to the great expansion in information on the subject which has occurred in recent years. This in turn is due primarily to previously inaccessible documentary and pictorial material from the former Eastern bloc, now that we have access to their archives. Such an undertaking now began to appear desirable and even necessary.

We were able to use my own work as the essential basis for the new volume, as this had recently borne fruit in the form of the book *Chronology of the War at Sea 1939 – 1945*, published in English by the London publishing house Greenhill and by the US Naval Institute Press. This work contains a wealth of names, dates and facts, and reflects the latest state of international research.

I am a historian, and as such have attempted in this book to describe to the reader and observer of the pictures the inter-related nature of the events in the Baltic and North Seas, in the Arctic, the Mediterranean, the Atlantic, the Indian Ocean and the Pacific. The book covers every aspect of the naval conflict, from the top-level discussions and decisions concerning technical requirements, to the battle events themselves, and, not least, their consequences for the people involved.

We are now dealing with events which occurred half a century ago. The number of those who experienced these events – or to be more precise survived them – is dwindling. It will not be long before nobody can actually tell from his own experience what the Second World War – the most terrible war in history – was really like. The purpose of this book soon became an attempt to give succeeding generations – amongst them future historians – some idea, however approximate, of how the war was enacted at sea. The publisher and I both participated in the naval war and as very young men experienced scenes which are not recorded in pictures at all. Why? Because in those moments when life and death were in the balance, nobody thought to pick up a camera. Incidentally, the German press and the weekly cinema news (television did not exist then) were forbidden to show pictures of dead German soldiers. As a result few people took such photographs, so the pictures which really reflect the brutal reality of war are notable by their absence in the archives. In contrast space could always be found in the press and at the cinema for the bemedalled aces who managed to shoot down aircraft and sink ships, even though they, like all soldiers, had no choice but to be potential perpetrators and victims alike.

For this very reason the publisher and I, as one-time witnesses, have taken much trouble to track down the relatively rare pictures from all the countries which were involved in the sea war, in an attempt to provide as truthful an impression of the events as possible. We have largely omitted pictures whose original purpose of glorification and propaganda is transparently obvious, and whose effect is to minimise the horror, death and misery which the war meant to those affected by it.

It has only been possible to bring this book to fruition with the willing help of individuals from many parts of the world. Their names are listed on the opposite page, and the publisher and I owe a grateful debt of thanks to every one.

Prof Dr Jürgen Rohwer
Stuttgart, October 1992

The Naval Arms Race

1922–1939/41

By the end of the First World War three of the eight great naval powers had been eliminated from the struggle for global or regional naval dominance. Austria-Hungary had disintegrated, and her multi-national fleet was divided up amongst the war's victorious powers, although only a few of the ships were absorbed into their fleets; the remainder being scrapped. In the disorder and confusion caused by the Civil War and Allied interventions, the Russian Baltic and Black Sea fleets were reduced to a minimal state. The German navy, whose most modern ships had been scuttled in Scapa Flow, was also obliged to surrender its surviving ships of relatively recent construction. In the Treaty of Versailles Germany was only permitted to retain six obsolescent battleships and six old cruisers (plus two more of each as reserves), twelve small destroyers and twelve torpedo boats (plus four each in reserve). She was denied the right to possess and build submarines and aircraft. For new vessels strict limits were laid down regarding tonnage, armament and contract dates. The most onerous restriction was in naval personnel, which was limited to 15,000 men.

The victorious powers were also faced with formidable problems. France and Italy had ceased building battleships and cruisers during the war, but those nations had been so severely weakened economically by the conflict that they were initially unable to resume the construction of these vessels. In fact, they were forced to abandon new vessels which were still building as well as those at the planning stage. Great Britain had been obliged to concentrate on building light units in an effort to combat the German U-boats, in addition to merchant ships to compensate for the losses during the second phase of the war, and for this reason had not been able to lay down any new major warships.

In contrast, the two non-European naval powers were in a more favourable position as the war had had less serious effects on them. After 1916 both countries had initiated major new shipbuilding programs making full use of their experience in the war. In 1916 the

USA's plan to build sixteen major warships and ten cruisers had been postponed in favour of destroyers and merchant ships, but in 1920 the programme was resumed with vigour. Japan viewed this plan as a threat, and countered it with what was known as the 8:8 programme, which foresaw the building of eight new super-battleships and eight battlecruisers by 1928 in addition to her existing ships.

However, in 1920/21 public opinion and governments generally were eager to reduce spending on armaments in view of the massive cost of the essential work required to repair the damage caused by the war. As a result, when the new US Secretary of External Affairs, Charles E Hughes, took the initiative of calling a conference aimed at limiting naval re-armament, the idea was broadly welcomed. Intensive negotiations were held at Washington, and eventually a treaty was signed which came into force on 6 February 1922. The right to keep existing possessions in the Pacific was guaranteed, the British-Japanese alliance was cancelled under the terms of the Four Power Treaty, and China's independence was recognised in the Nine Power Treaty. In addition to these measures a Fleet Treaty was agreed between Great Britain, USA, Japan, France and Italy, laying down a strength ratio of 5 : 5 : 3 : 1.75 : 1.75. Battleship tonnage was restricted to 525,000 tons for Great Britain and USA, 315,000 tons for Japan and 175,000 tons each for France and Italy. The building of replacement vessels could not commence for a further twenty years, and these were to be no larger than 35,000 tons with a maximum armament of 16in guns. To compensate for the technical obsolescence of the older British units compared with the new American and Japanese ships, Great Britain was permitted to build two new battleships.

Aircraft carriers were limited to 27,000 tons and 8in guns. Of the new American and Japanese battlecruisers which were to be scrapped both countries were permitted to convert two vessels into aircraft carriers. Great Britain was building no ships of this

type, and had to be content with the conversion of her 'large light cruisers'.

Money-saving measures and the provisions of the Washington Treaty actually resulted in the scrapping of forty-six of Great Britain's pre-dreadnought battleships and large armoured cruisers. The corresponding figures for other countries were USA: twenty-three, Japan: nine, France: thirteen, and Italy: nine. In terms of dreadnoughts and battlecruisers the numbers were eighteen for Great Britain and three each for USA and Japan. Of the super-battleships under construction at that time eleven were broken up in the USA and four in Japan, and two further vessels were converted to aircraft carriers in each country. Great Britain abandoned the building of four battlecruisers, Japan waived eight further planned ships, and France and Italy both decided not to resume work on four halted battleships, although France did complete one new ship as an aircraft carrier.

Since the Treaty forbade the construction of new battleships, the naval armaments race soon shifted to the building of cruisers, whose maximum size had been laid down at 10,000 tons with 8in guns. The consequence of this trend was a demand for further treaties to limit naval re-armament. Initial negotiations were held in Geneva, but they failed because Great Britain and USA could not agree on the size and number of cruisers to be allowed. Japan pressed for an increase in her quota from 60 to 70 per cent. Neither France nor Italy was satisfied with their equal standing at 35 per cent. France would not agree to a British appeal to ban submarines.

The London Treaty of 22 April 1930, which France and Italy did not sign, restricted the number of battleships to fifteen each for Great Britain and the USA, and to nine for Japan, and extended the building moratorium until 1936. A compromise was agreed concerning cruisers which involved dividing them into heavy and light vessels with the dividing line set at a gun calibre of 6in. This clause allowed the USA eighteen ships,

The German 'pocket battleship' *Deutschland* fitting out at Kiel in 1932

Great Britain fifteen and Japan twelve. Compensation was planned for light cruisers. Limits were laid down for the tonnage and size of destroyers and submarines, and the building of aircraft carriers of less than 10,000 tons was forbidden. No restrictions were placed on vessels displacing less than 600 tons and ships up to 2,000 tons provided that they were fitted with no guns larger than 6in, no more than four 3in guns, no torpedo tubes and had a top speed of no more than 20 knots.

An attempt was made to soften the effects of naval armaments limitation by means of a further London Treaty, but it failed. The treaty signed on 25 March 1936 by Great Britain, USA and France only added qualitative restrictions concerning the size and gun calibre of the warship categories already defined, but did not establish ton-

nage ratios between the powers. Great Britain strove to include other nations by means of bi-lateral agreements. A treaty signed with Germany in 1935 fixed the strength of her fleet at 35 per cent of the British one, and in 1937 another treaty was concluded which caused the Soviet Union to acknowledge the definition of terms. But without Japan and Italy, and with various loopholes in the treaties, the restrictions on maritime armament had become a farce. A new naval arms race had begun.

One of the first steps in the new arms race was the laying down of the German armoured ship *Deutschland*, pictured above fitting out in Kiel in 1932. This vessel did not fit into the categories laid down by the Treaties of Washington and London, and France responded by building her own fast battleship. Italy in turn reacted by starting

work on her first new 35,000-ton battleship. Germany's rejection of the Versailles limitations, the Japanese and Italian revocation of the Fleet Treaties, and the aggressive policies of these nations, forced the USA, Great Britain and France to adopt new fleet building programmes, each action causing a more strenuous reaction. At the same time the Soviet Union felt threatened first by England and then by Japan and Germany, and the Spanish Civil War exposed Soviet naval weakness to such an extent, that she initiated a gigantic expansion of her maritime power.

The cruiser size limitation set by the 1922 Washington Treaty was based on the largest new cruiser type of that time: the British Hawkins class. These vessels had a standard displacement of 9,550 to 9,860 tons, ie just under 10,000 tons, and were armed with 7.5in guns, although the Washington Treaty agreed on the internationally more common 8in calibre as the limit for cruiser armament.

Since battleships could not be built until 1936, the focus of warship building shifted to what became known as the 'Washington' cruiser. The type met the American and Japanese need for large cruisers with trans-Pacific range, while Great Britain was interested in building up the maximum number of smaller cruisers for her Empire and trade

protection obligations, as these vessels were able to rely upon a world-wide network of bases.

Between 1924 and 1926 all five great naval powers made plans to build series of these 10,000-ton 'Washington' cruisers: by 1927/28 Great Britain had ordered thirteen County class ships, in the USA initial contracts were granted for eight ships of the Pensacola and Northampton classes, followed by a further nine in 1930/31, and in 1935 one final 10,000-ton cruiser. The photograph here shows the Northampton class *Louisville* fitting out in 1930, with the aircraft carrier *Lexington* in the background. Japan started by building four smaller 8in cruisers, then followed with eight ships of the

Nachi and Takao classes. France and Italy each laid down seven of these units, which after 1930 were known as heavy cruisers.

With the restrictions placed on these 10,000-ton cruisers in London in 1930 the focus of cruiser construction shifted to ships with 6in guns, although most of them were scarcely smaller than the heavy cruisers. The Japanese Mogami class ships were followed by the British Southamptons and the American Brooklyns, all displacing 9,000 to 10,000 tons and carrying twelve or fifteen 6in guns. France and Italy turned to smaller, faster units, and the new treaty-limited German cruisers were also similar. In 1936 a tonnage limit of 8,000 tons had been decreed, but it was widely ignored.

US cruiser *Louisville* refitting 1930. Aircraft carrier *Lexington* in background.

Battleship HMS *Warspite* in dock 1934.

The Washington Treaty had permitted the maritime powers to modernise older battleships, and had also allowed for a 3,000-ton increase in displacement for these ships by the addition of side bulges, extra armour and improved propulsion systems. This clause was exploited by all the leading navies, and resulted in extensive refits which almost amounted to completely new vessels in some cases. Japan in particular sought to compensate for her inferiority in numerical terms by implementing massive improvements in armour protection, in heavy gun range and in speed.

The French considered her older ships to be unsuitable for extensive modernisation work, but the Americans thought differently. After, initially, limited work on her older ships, in 1930 the USA began a programme of more fundamental refits typified by the New Mexico class, which gained better underwater protection, improved propulsion systems and stronger armour protection. In Great Britain the major emphasis was initially aimed at making up for the defects which had become apparent in the Battle of Jutland, but in 1934 work began on a more extensive refit to *Warspite*, as shown in the photograph here. The ship is shown still in the dockyard, where primarily the horizontal armour and anti-aircraft defensive measures were improved. Before her sisterships were complete, the war had begun.

The German armoured ships, or pocket battleships as they were known, which lay outside the provisions of the fleet treaties, were fitted with 11in guns and were thus superior to the Washington cruisers. The response of other nations to these vessels was to build high-speed 'anti-pocket battleships'. In France, where it had been permissible to build replacement battleships after 1927, work began in 1931 on the 26,500-ton *Dunkerque*, which had a top speed of 29.5 knots and eight 13in guns, mounted in two turrets forward after the pattern of the British *Nelson*. In the picture at top left the *Dunkerque*'s sistership *Strasbourg* is shown on the stocks. Germany in turn converted its planned 20,000-ton armoured ships into the fast *Scharnhorst* and *Gneisenau* battleships displacing 32,100 tons, with a top speed of 31 knots and nine 11in guns.

Since the mid-thirties the Soviet Union had been drawing up plans for a 'Washington cruiser hunter' of 23,000 tons with 10in guns, but in 1937 a battlecruiser was designed in response to the *Scharnhorst*, displacing 35,240 tons, with a speed of 32 knots and nine 12in guns, and no fewer than sixteen units of the type were to be built by 1947. The picture shows the second ship *Sevastopol* on the stocks in Nikolayev in 1941. In Germany the Z-plan was being implemented, providing for twelve armoured ships of 22,145 tons, but in 1939 the plan was dropped in favour of three battlecruisers of 28,900 tons with a top speed of 33.5 knots, armed with six 15in guns. Although these ships were cancelled in September of the same year, a German-Soviet treaty was signed in 1940 which led to the modification of the Soviet battlecruisers which were already building to incorporate German 15in turrets and German fire control systems. In 1940 the Americans finalised plans to build six battlecruisers of the Alaska type (29,000 tons), and the Japanese had plans to build corresponding designs.

The construction of destroyers had primarily been the province of France, Italy and Japan, where two parallel series of large (up to 2,400 tons) and smaller (around 1,300 tons) destroyers were built. After 1930 Great Britain, USA, Japan and the Soviet Union made great efforts to recapture lost ground, while France, Italy and Germany started building smaller torpedo boats of around 1,000 tons in addition to large destroyers.

(top) *Strasbourg*.

(left) Russian battlecruiser *Sevastopol* under construction.

In the 1920s France attempted to compensate for her weakness in surface ships by building up a powerful submarine force of large ocean-going vessels. Amongst these was *Le Centaure*, shown below launching on 14 October 1932. Japan and the USA also began to build large submarines for fleet operations, and Great Britain built patrol boats as replacements for the Far Eastern battlefleet. After 1930 Italy and Germany also took up submarine building, but they were overshadowed by the Soviet effort, where many submarines were built. The picture shows the first Soviet Black Sea submarine D-4 on a visit to Istanbul on 18 October 1933.

(right) Russian submarine *D-4* in Istanbul harbour.

(below) Launch of French submarine *Le Centaure*.

Although submarines and aircraft were fated eventually to become the focal point of naval warfare, until the Second World War it was the battleships which remained the core of the national fleets, and the yardstick by which a maritime power was judged. By the Washington Treaty France and Italy had been permitted 70,000 tons each after 1927 for new ships to replace their obsolescent battleships. In Italy plans were drawn up for three ships of 23,000 tons, but they were discarded as inadequate. Instead the Italians decided in 1934 to convert the four old Cavour class vessels into modern light battleships, and to build two 35,000-ton ships in response to the French *Dunkerque*. One of these was the *Vittorio Veneto* shown here fit-ting out in 1939. In 1935 the construction of 35,000-ton battleships began to increase at an alarming rate, and this size was being exceeded even before the tonnage limit was raised to 45,000 tons in 1938: in 1935 France granted contracts for two Richelieu class ships (38,500 tons) followed by a further two in 1938. Italy responded in 1938 with two fur-ther Littorio class ships (41,200 tons). In 1935 Germany started work on two Bismarck class vessels (41,700 tons), while Great Britain began building five King George Vs (38,000 tons) in 1936/37. In the USA two North Carolinas and four South Dakotas (each 38,000 tons) were on the stocks in 1937/38. The Japanese, who had withdrawn from the treaties, awarded building contracts for four Yamato class ships (65,000 tons) in 1937 and 1939, while the Soviet Union finalised plans to build no fewer than fifteen Sovietskiy Soyuz's (59,150 tons) in 1938, of which the first three were actually started. Great Britain ordered four Lions (40,000 tons) in 1938/39, the USA six Iowas (48,500 tons) in 1939/40 and five Montanas (60,500 tons) in 1940 while the German Z-plan included ships H to N (52,600 tons). Only four of the Iowa class ships were completed, the others abandoned.

In contrast the number of aircraft carri-ers included in the building programmes was quite small; by the outbreak of war Great Britain was building eight, the USA four, Japan five, France two and Germany two.

Italian battleship *Vittorio Veneto* completing 1939.

Schleswig-Holstein bombarding Polish fortifications.

The German Offensives
1 September 1939–30 June 1940

At 0445hrs on 1 September 1939 the German attack on Poland began, unleashing Hitler's war of conquest aimed at gaining Lebensraum – space for living. It was to grow into a world war lasting six years in which more than 55 million people were to lose their lives.

The photograph above shows the German battleship *Schleswig-Holstein* (see page 2) in Danzig-Neufahrwasser, where it had arrived six days previously for a friendly visit. The ship is firing its 11in turrets at the fortified Polish Westerplatte close by. These were the first shots of the war, and at the same time they signalled the start of the naval war which eventually spread to encom-

pass all the world's oceans. For seven days the Polish defenders of the Westerplatte repulsed the massive German attacks.

As early as 30 August the three service-able Polish destroyers had put to sea making for England, and the five submarines took up position outside the Bay of Danzig. Their attempts at attacking the German forces, which were initially extremely powerful, failed just as completely as did the German efforts to hunt the submarines by destroyers, minesweepers and U-boats. The Polish warships and merchant ships lying in the ports of Gdingen and Hela were destroyed by bombs from German bombers and dive bombers. The more modern German ships and U-boats

were soon withdrawn to the West, while the two old battleships and the minesweepers used their guns to support the army troops which were attempting to push forward from Danzig towards Gdingen and the Hela peninsula. It was not until 1 October that the first German ship was lost, when the minesweeper *M 85* ran onto a Polish submarine-laid mine off Heisternest. Twenty-four members of the crew died when the ship sank. Of the Polish submarines three entered Swedish ports in the second half of September when their supplies were exhausted, and allowed themselves to be interned. Two broke through to England.

Polish prisoners from the Westplatte.

(right) German torpedo-boat loaded with mines for the east coast of England 1940.

The battle for Poland would eventually come to an end in the same region when, five and a half years later, the last serviceable German destroyers, torpedo boats and S-boats evacuated 43,000 men on the day of the German surrender from the Hela peninsula outside the Bay of Danzig. On 7 September 1939 the defenders of the Westerplatte were forced to abandon their resistance and, as depicted here, taken prisoner; but 4,000 men on Hela carried on fighting until 1 October, when they were the last Polish troops to surrender.

Poland was divided up between Germany and the Soviet Union, whose troops had marched into Eastern Poland on 17 September. There was now a single Western

land front where the British and French opposed the Germans, the British having declared war on 3 September. This situation, the 'phoney war', in which no major operations were carried out, was to last seven months.

The circumstances of the war at sea were very different, where there was no rest. Mines became the centre of attention. In September German cruisers, mine-layers, destroyers and torpedo boats laid the defensive blockade system known as the Westwall to secure the German Bight. After a dense network of mine barrages had been laid in the Dover Straits the British Admiralty declared a strip of sea off the east coast as a

declared minefield area in order to protect British shipping. From October 1939 until February 1940 German destroyers laid large numbers of mines off the English east coast in a series of seven offensive operations, supplemented by barrages laid by U-boats and dropped by the Luftwaffe. Three British destroyers and eighty-two merchant ships fell victim to these mines. Whilst attempting to evade bombs dropped by their own aircraft two German destroyers ran onto British mines and sank with a total loss of 590 men. The picture on the right shows a German torpedo boat loaded with mines.

During the seven months of the 'phoney war' both sides attacked merchant shipping and took prizes. Starting in mid-September 1939 German destroyers and torpedo boats monitored neutral shipping in the Kattegat and Skagerrak. By 3 October they had stopped 130 ships and captured twenty-one of them as prizes. After early October minelayers and patrol boats were set to work in the Baltic to check merchant shipping and by the end of October had forced 127 ships into Kiel and Swinemünde. The top photograph shows a prize command from the German destroyer *Hans Lody* examining the Danish steamer *Aslaug* for contraband.

During September the British Home Fleet carried out several operations in the hunt for German blockade-runners. On 6 September the Northern Patrol was established between Iceland and the Orkneys, with the purpose of examining neutral ships. Initially, the patrol consisted of old cruisers, but later large passenger ships were employed, fitted out as auxiliary cruisers. These vessels possessed better range in the rough conditions. By the end of October they had captured eight blockade-runners and stopped 283 merchant ships, of which seventy-one were brought in to Kirkwall in the Orkneys. In the lower picture neutral merchant ships are seen anchored off a British port, waiting to be checked for contraband.

In a drive against the Northern Patrol in November, the German battleships *Scharnhorst* and *Gneisenau* sank the auxiliary cruiser *Rawalpindi*.

The British attempted to disrupt German shipping along the Norwegian coast and in the German Bight with submarines, but the operation was abandoned in January 1940 after a few minor successes when German minesweepers sank three of the submarines within a few days.

(above left) Boat from German destroyer *Hans Lody* rowing to inspect Danish merchantman for contraband.

(left) Neutral merchant ships in a British port for contraband checks.

HMS *Glowworm* sunk by *Admiral Hipper*.

The Winter War, started by the Soviet attack on Finland on 30 November 1939, forced military chiefs to turn their attention increasingly towards Scandinavia. The attack by the British destroyer *Cossack* on the German supply ship *Altmark* in the Norwegian Jössingfjord, carried out with the aim of rescuing 303 seamen captured from merchant ships which had been sunk by the armoured ship *Admiral Graf Spee*, compelled the Germans to bring forward their plans to occupy Norway. Germany was importing crucial supplies of ore from Sweden, carried by sea from the north Norwegian ports, and to stop this traffic England planned minelaying operations along the Norwegian coast as well as troop landings to ward off German landings.

On 7 April 1940 the entire German fleet, divided into eleven groups and carrying troops, put to sea with the aim of conquering Denmark and Norway. At the same time British destroyers were making for Bodø and Kristiansund for a minelaying operation. In a severe storm the destroyer *Glowworm* lost contact with the task group led by the battle-cruiser *Renown*, and ran into the German Trondheim group. After a violent battle in which the two ships collided, the cruiser *Admiral Hipper* set the *Glowworm* on fire, shown in the photograph above. *Glowworm* sank, but the Home Fleet had put to sea in the meantime, and a group of fast ships was dispatched towards the *Renown* in response to the *Glowworm*'s emergency signal.

On 9 April, before these ships arrived, a brief battle took place between the *Renown* and the battleships *Scharnhorst* and *Gneisenau* off the Lofotens, where the German ships had been cruising to cover the Narvik operation. By this time ten German destroyers had been able to capture Narvik with the mountain troops that they carried on board.

Landings by German troops in Trondheim, Bergen, Kristiansund/Arendal, Egersund and certain Danish ports were also successful, encountering little in the way of resistance. The only exception was the loss of the newly-built heavy cruiser *Blücher* in the Oslofjord, sunk by artillery fire and torpedoes from the Norwegian coastal battery at Oscarsborg in the Dröbaks narrows. Three hundred and twenty seamen and soldiers met their deaths in the sinking.

(left) German cruiser *Königsberg* sunk by British dive-bombers at Bergen.

(top) Chaos caused by British destroyers' torpedo attack in Narvik fjörd.

(above) German *Lützow* damaged astern by British submarine.

On 10 April 1940 a massive British counter-attack began. Five destroyers carried out a surprise attack on the port of Narvik in the grey dawn and driving snow and caused havoc with their torpedoes (top photograph). On the same day fifteen British dive bombers of the Fleet Air Arm attacked the cruiser *Königsberg* lying at Bergen and did so much damage that the vessel went up in flames and sank (photo left). British submarines were also successful in the Skagerrak. On 11 April they sank the cruiser *Karlsruhe* and several transports, and severely damaged the stern of the pocket battleship *Lützow*, as shown in the lower photograph.

Early on 13 April 1940 the British battleship *Warspite* and nine destroyers, amongst them the *Punjabi* and *Eskimo* (pictured left) entered Ofotfjord in driving snow and destroyed the remaining German destroyers at Narvik. The photograph beneath shows the *Bernd von Armin* after running aground in the Rombaksfjord.

The picture on the right shows German sailors at the grave of a fallen comrade at Narvik. 435 Norwegians, 321 Germans and 188 Britons fell in the sea battles on 10 and 13 April. In total, the Norwegian operation accounted for 5,300 German deaths.

From 13 April convoys carrying British infantry brigades, French Alpine troops and Polish troops put to sea making for Norway, and landed the troops at Namsos, Andalsnes and Harstad. In the photograph below an English troop transport approaches Norway as part of a French convoy.

(top left) HMS *Punjabi* and *Eskimo* in the Ofotfjord.
(bottom left) *Bernd von Arnim* in the Rombaksfjord.
(right) German sailors at Narvik.
(below) A British troopship en route to Norway.

(top left) Cruiser HMS *Vindictive* bombed by German aircraft in the Ofotfjord.

(bottom left) British troop transport *Orama* sinking.

(above) German fleet off Trondheim: *Gneisnau* (foreground), *Scharnhorst* (behind) and *Admiral Hipper* (right).

After 29 April 1940 the Allies were forced to evacuate Andalsnes and Namsos and accept losses, but the battle for Narvik, defended by mountain troops and sailors from the sunken German destroyers, continued under the harshest of conditions. Again and again British and Polish ships entered the the fjord, bombarded the town and landed troops. The top photograph left shows the British cruiser *Vindictive* in the Ofotfjord, in a hail of bombs from German aircraft. The Allies eventually captured Narvik on 28 May, but they found themselves unable to hold it. During the evacuation operation the German fleet (in the photograph above, taken at Trondheim in June, *Gneisenau* is in the foreground, with *Scharnhorst* behind and *Admiral Hipper* on the right) had a number of successes: the troop transport *Orama* (pictured left) and the aircraft carrier *Glorious* were sunk by two destroyers.

In the meantime the German Western offensive had forced Holland and Belgium to surrender and the British Expeditionary Force found itself surrounded at Dunkerque together with the remainder of the French 1st Army. Between 28 May and 4 June 1940, 848 allied ships ranging from destroyers to small motor boats evacuated 338,226 men to England in Operation Dynamo, under constant attack by the Luftwaffe. The photograph on left shows the French destroyer *Bourrasque* off Niewpoort on 30 May, sunk by artillery fire, while below British destroyers are shown landing evacuated soldiers at Dover. Thirty thousand Englishmen and fifty thousand Frenchmen died or were taken prisoner.

(left) French destroyer *Bourrasque* sunk by artillery off Nieuwpoort.

(below) British destroyers landing evacuees from Dunkirk at Dover May/June 1940.

Barges assembled for 'Operation Sealion' in Boulogne harbour.

On 25 June 1940 the armistice with France came into effect, and the German Command staff then began to make serious plans for an invasion of England – Operation Sealion. In July a broad-based landing was being considered; this was the option preferred by the army, but the navy considered it impractical. While the dispute was being settled, army pioneers, the navy and the Luftwaffe worked all-out to improvise the landing vessels required, using requisitioned freighters, fishing vessels and, in particular, inland tugs and barges. By August these vessels had been grouped together in the Channel ports, as can be seen in this aerial photograph, showing Sealion barges in Boulogne harbour. British aerial attacks and gunfire from the sea had their effect, and forced the Germans to disband the concentrations of ships. However, the crucial factor in the cancellation of the landing in September 1940 was the defeat of the Luftwaffe in the Battle of Britain.

Battle of the Atlantic I

1 September 1939–30 June 1940

(top left) US freighter *City of Flint* photographed from *Deutschland*.

(bottom left) *Graf Spee* scuttled in the River Plate.

(above) HMS *Exeter* returns.

On 21 and 24 August 1939 the German Naval Command allowed the pocket battleships *Admiral Graf Spee* and *Deutschland* to put to sea and take up waiting positions in the Atlantic together with their supply ships *Altmark* and *Westerwald*. However, although war had been declared on 3 September, the reluctance of France and England lead to delaying orders and prevented them going into action until 26 September. On 30 September they sank their first ships in the Atlantic, and eight British-French battle formations took up the hunt for them.

On 9 October the *Deutschland* stopped the American freighter *City of Flint* (shown top left and photographed from the *Deutschland*). Commanded by a prize crew the ship was intended to steam to Germany via Murmansk, but it was requisitioned by the Norwegians and handed back to the Americans. In the meantime the *Graf Spee* had sunk four ships on the Capetown – Freetown route before entering the Indian Ocean. There she sank two further ships, returned to the South Atlantic, took supplies, and continued to sink more ships.

On 13 December 1939 the *Graf Spee* was hunted down off La Plata by a British cruis-er group consisting of the *Exeter*, *Ajax* and *Achilles*. The picture above shows the *Exeter* enjoying an exultant welcome after returning home with temporary repairs to her severe battle damage. In the battle seventy-two men died on the British cruisers and thirty-six on the *Graf Spee*. The damaged *Graf Spee* ran into the neutral port of Montevideo where it was established that she could not be restored to battle-worthy condition there. Accordingly, the ship was taken out to sea and there scuttled by her own crew on 17 December at La Plata, depicted in the lower photograph on the left.

(above) *Bremen* entering New York harbour.

(left) German freighter *Watussi* on fire.

In accordance with the treaties already concluded, the Soviet Union granted to Germany the Basis Nord in a bay near Murmansk, and by 18 September 1939 eighteen merchant ships had gathered there after breaking through the British blockade, amongst them the fast steamer *Bremen*, which had passed through the Denmark strait from New York unnoticed by the British. The top photograph shows the crew singing the national anthem on deck after arriving in New York, while the top picture opposite shows the port wing of the ship's bridge as she runs into Murmansk. However, many of the German blockade-runners fell victim to the British and French hunter groups on the open sea, including the *Watussi*. The ship was spotted by a South African aircraft on 2 December, then scuttled and abandoned by her crew (pictured left) when the cruiser *Sussex* and the battlecruiser *Renown* approached.

At President Roosevelt's instigation the US Navy's neutrality patrol set up the Pan-American security zone on 2 October 1939, extending to the west of 60° West and 300 nautical miles off South America. The neutrality patrol monitored the actions of the warring nations and reported them by radio. In practice, these operations were directed against German ships. For example, the passenger steamer *Columbus* was accompanied by ten destroyers from Vera Cruz to west of Florida, the ships steaming in pairs and taking over from each other, until on 19 December the cruiser *Tuscaloosa* led the British destroyer *Hyperion* to the ship with its signals. The crew of the *Columbus* was obliged to set the ship alight and abandon it, as shown in the photograph below. About a year later the freighter *Idarwald* suffered the same fate off Cuba, and was forced to scuttle herself at the approach of the British cruiser *Diomede* which had been led to her by the Americans.

(right) Bremen arriving at Murmansk.

(below) Crew of *Columbus* abandoning ship.

As early as 19 August 1939 the German Naval Command had sent fourteen U-boats out into the Atlantic with the aim of capturing merchant shipping using prize crews as soon as the war started. On 3 September *U 30* sank the passenger steamer *Athenia*, which it considered to be an auxiliary cruiser, and of the 1,400 passengers 112 died, amongst them 28 Americans. The British assumed that Germany had already initiated an unrestricted submarine war, and began to prepare convoys and form hunter formations based on aircraft carriers. On 14 September *U 39* was sunk by destroyers after a failed attack on the aircraft carrier *Ark Royal*, but on 17 September *U 29* torpedoed the aircraft carrier *Courageous* and sank her (right), taking 514 seamen to the bottom.

(right) HMS *Courageous* hit by *U 29*'s torpedoes.

(below) *U 47* and the cruiser *Emden*.

On 5 September the U-boats began the merchant war in the Atlantic under prize regulations. By early October the Germans had taken twenty-eight of the ships they had stopped as prizes after checking their documents. Three of them were brought back to Germany, and the others were sunk after allowing the crews to launch the lifeboats. Crews were often given course directions and emergency supplies. A typical example was the capture by *U 48* of the British freighter *Royal Sceptre* on 5 September, which a crew member recorded in the photographs reproduced here. In the top photograph one of the freighter's boats comes alongside *U 48* with the ship's papers, while below the steamer is sunk by gunfire and torpedo, and in the bottom photograph members of the crew of the merchant ship take their leave in a lifeboat.

In the meantime the small Type II U-boats had been busy in the North Sea, laying magnetic mines in the bays and river estuaries of the English east coast. Larger U-boats were also employed in the Channel and off the west coast for similar mine operations, and by June 1940 forty-two ships totalling 57,760grt had fallen victim to the mines.

As in the First World War, when three British armoured cruisers were sunk by *U 9*, the world's attention was caught by a single U-boat operation on 14 October 1939, when *U 47* penetrated into the strongly secured main British base of Scapa Flow and sank the battleship *Royal Oak*. The *Royal Oak* knew nothing of the initial attack which failed due to a malfunctioning torpedo. On the return of *U 47* to Wilhelmshaven, the submarine was enthusiastically greeted by the crews of other warships (pictured on the left with the cruiser *Emden*). On her conning tower is the boat's commander, Kapitänleutnant Prien, known as the 'bull of Scapa Flow'. The Home Fleet was forced to transfer to Loch Ewe for a few weeks, where the battleship *Nelson* suffered serious damage after striking a magnetic mine laid by *U 31*. The newly-built cruiser *Belfast* was also severely damaged by a mine laid by *U 21* in the Firth of Forth, while the battleship *Barham* was torpedoed and damaged by *U 30* off the Hebrides in late December. By this time nine German U-boats had been lost with a total of 204 men, and 144 men had been taken prisoner.

U 48 sinks the *Royal Sceptre*: *(top)* boat carrying ship's papers alongside *U 48*; *(middle) Royal Sceptre* sunk by gunfire and torpedo; *(bottom) Royal Sceptre*'s crew in lifeboat.

(above) Gun being fitted to British merchant ship.

(left) A destroyer speaking to a merchant ship.

The British Admiralty now began to arm merchant ships in an attempt to ward off German U-boats. The photograph above shows the improvised base at the stern of a freighter with armament being installed.

The Admiralty's 'Trade Division' now took over the checking and control of merchant shipping. In the picture on the left an officer on a destroyer gives directions to a merchant ship by megaphone. Around this time British merchant ships were ordered to broadcast an 'SSS' message by radio if they sighted a U-boat, and an attempt was to be made to ram the submarine. As a result the U-boats found it increasingly difficult to capture merchant ships and install a prize command. The German response was to expand the approved areas where U-boats were able to attack without warning.

On 17 August 1940 Germany declared a wide sea area around England to be an operational area in which ships encountered would be sunk without warning.

In response the British began to concentrate increasingly on grouping ships together in convoys. The photograph below shows the new corvette *Hibiscus* in the summer of 1940 on convoy escort duty. Since a German invasion was expected, many destroyers had to be kept in reserve to ward off that eventuality, and as a result the convoys were poorly protected. At Churchill's request Roosevelt lent to England fifty old destroyers on 2 September 1940 as part of the Destroyer Naval Base Deal, in exchange for naval bases in the Caribbean. These ships were employed to reinforce the convoys after the end of 1940. One of them was the destroyer *St. Croix* (ex USS *McCook*), by this time a Canadian vessel, which is seen on the right shortly after her transfer.

(below) New corvette HMS *Hibiscus*.　　*(above)* Canadian *St. Croix* (ex-US *McCook*).

Battle of the Atlantic II

1 July 1940–11 December 1941

(left) German auxiliary cruiser *Pinguin* transferring torpedo to *UA* (ex-Turkish *Batiray*).

(above) *U 30* being guided into Lorient.

With the conquest of Norway and the French west coast the German navy gained a number of new bases. *U 30* was the first U-boat to be based in one of these ports, and is shown above on 7 July 1940 being guided into harbour off Lorient by a minesweeper.

Until this time the U-boats had taken about a week to travel from the German Bight into the operational region to the west of the English Channel or the Bay of Biscay, but the journey from the new bases to the British shipping routes, grouped together in the northern part of the Channel, scarcely took longer than two days. In August the U-boats attacked numerous convoys, which were still poorly guarded, although there were seldom more than ten U-boats in the operational area at any one time. Lone merchant ships became an increasingly uncommon sight.

During this period the first long-range operations were carried out off the West African coast. The large submarine *Batiray* had been under construction at Kiel for the Turks, but in September 1939 was requisitioned and subsequently put to sea from Kiel as *UA*. She sank the auxiliary cruiser *Andania* of the Northern Patrol after the ship had been picked up by German radio intelligence, and then travelled to the Cape Verdes region and reached Freetown. The photograph on the left shows the U-boat *UA* in mid-Atlantic on 18 July 1940 taking on supplies and transferring a torpedo from the auxiliary cruiser *Pinguin*. After sinking seven ships totalling 40,706 BRT *UA* returned to Lorient on 28 August after an operational voyage lasting eighty-two days. *U 65* followed her out and stayed at sea from October to January 1941, sinking eight ships

with a total tonnage of 47,785 BRT and torpedoing one other.

The U-boat operations were supported by the German radio decoding service, the xB-Dienst, which had succeeded in breaking into the two British navy radio codes which used code books superenciphered by long subtractor tables. A change in the code documents on 20th August brought a halt to the xB-Dienst successes for a time.

The small number of U-boats available made it difficult to locate the convoys and hindered the radio-guided operations from the U-boat command which had been transferred to Kernevel near Lorient. Its task was to direct groups of U-boats to the convoys. The navy tried to deploy long-range reconnaissance aircraft with the help of the Luftwaffe, but the attempt was not successful until January 1941.

In September 1940 German U-boats began to attack convoys using land-based directions. The first attempt was against the convoy SC.2 which had been reported by the German xB-Dienst, and four U-boats were sent in to the attack. Five ships were sunk, to the surprise of the the British Admiralty, who were not expecting the U-boats to attack at night while on the surface. In such an action the Asdic underwater sound location system was of no use at all, in spite of the great expectations for the device. The photograph on the left shows a stricken steamer during a night attack in the autumn of 1940.

German U-boats were sent far out west into the Atlantic to gather weather reports for the planned Operation Sealion, and on 20 September one of these submarines picked up the convoy HX.72 consisting of forty-one ships. The U-boat directed four other submarines to the convoy, and they sank a total of twelve ships. In the period from 17 to 20 October an even greater success was achieved when ten U-boats destroyed twenty-one ships from the convoy SC.7 followed by twelve ships from HX.79, without being seriously endangered in any way by the escort vessels.

It was not until late 1940, when it was acknowledged in England that the expected German invasion had obviously been cancelled, that it was possible to reinforce the convoy escort systems, and from this time on it became more difficult for the U-boats to get into attack positions.

In the period August to October the Italian navy sent twenty-seven of its larger submarines into the Atlantic to reinforce the small number of German U-boats. They were based at Bordeaux and operated in conjunction with the German U-boats. The top photograph shows one of the Italian submarines putting to sea for an Atlantic operation in the Bay of Biscay. The Italians found the conditions in the Atlantic unfamiliar and also lacked expertise in ocean operations, and it was not until some of the Italian commanders had trained on German submarines that they began to have some success.

The Germans had to wait until the spring of 1941 for the number of U-boats stationed in France to rise significantly with the arrival of newly-built vessels. The bottom photograph shows four new U-boats in a French Atlantic port.

(left) Merchant ship under U-boat attack at night.

(top right) Italian submarine heading into Atlantic.

(bottom right) Four new U-boats in a French port.

By the autumn of 1940 the heavy German surface ships had been repaired to the point where they were able to put to sea one after the other for their planned operations in the war against merchant shipping.

The *Admiral Scheer* was the first ship to reach the North Atlantic on 6 November, where she attacked the convoy HX.84. It took a protracted battle to sink the escorting

(top left) Admiral Scheer.

(below far left) Ship of Convoy SLS 64.

(below left) Survivors boarding Gneisenau.

(below) Scharnhorst in the Atlantic.

British auxiliary cruiser *Jervis Bay*, and this gave the thirty-seven ships time to disperse, so the German ship was only able to sink five vessels. The *Admiral Scheer* then headed for the South Atlantic and into the Indian Ocean. The top photograph shows her seen from a British merchant ship which she had captured. On 1 April 1941 she returned after sinking seventeen ships.

The *Admiral Hipper* passed through the Denmark Straits in early December 1940 and entered Brest on 27 December after a brief battle with the cruiser escort of a troop transport convoy. On a further voyage in February 1941 she attacked the convoy

SLS.64 which had set out from Freetown, and sank seven ships (one of which is shown in flames in the lower picture), before she broke through to Norway after a brief stop in Brest.

The *Scharnhorst* and *Gneisenau* steamed through the Denmark Straits to reach the Atlantic, where in a period of two months they sank or captured twenty-two ships from dispersed convoys and individual vessels. On 23 March 1941 both ships entered Brest. The picture below shows the *Scharnhorst* in mid-Atlantic, while in the facing picture the *Gneisenau* takes on board survivors of an allied freighter she had just sunk.

For the German heavy units and auxiliary cruisers to operate successfully they required reliable support, and thus the supply ships sent out into the Atlantic for them had a crucial role to play. Occasionally, auxiliary cruisers were pressed into service to supply the U-boats in mid-Atlantic, as for example the auxiliary cruiser *Pinguin* pic-

tured below camouflaged as the Greek freighter *Kassos* (below), and the auxiliary cruiser *Kormoran*, shown on the right refuelling a U-boat. This picture was taken in mid-Atlantic.

(below) German auxiliary cruiser *Pinguin* disguised as Greek freighter *Kassos*.

(bottom) *Carnarvon Castle* at Rio de Janeiro showing battle damage.

U-boat refuelling from auxiliary cruiser *Kormoran* in mid-Atlantic.

From late March to early December 1940 the German auxiliary cruisers *Atlantis, Orion, Widder, Thor, Pinguin* and *Kormoran* put to sea one after the other and steamed through the Denmark Straits into the Atlantic, always under cover of a new moon, unnoticed by the enemy. In the summer of 1940 the *Komet* made its way out using the northeast passage around Siberia, with the help of Soviet icebreakers. Naval Command used radio signals to control the actions of the auxiliary cruisers in the operational areas of mid- and South Atlantic, the Indian Ocean and the Pacific. The auxiliary cruisers were camouflaged as Allied or neutral merchant ships,

and approached any ship once detected, dropped the camouflage at the last moment, hoisted the German ensign and stopped the ship with a shot across the bow. If the vessel hove to, a prize command was sent on board to examine the ship's papers and cargo. If the ship had contraband on board the crew would be taken prisoner and the ship sunk or sent to France with a prize crew. However, many ships followed the orders of the British Admiralty and broadcast RRR ('Raider') signals, in which case the auxiliary cruiser would open fire directly.

Once the Allied forces recognised the presence of a raider, cruisers or hunter

groups were sent to the attack. In July and December 1940 the *Thor* managed to escape from attacks by the British auxiliary cruisers *Alcantara* and *Carnarvon Castle*; the picture at bottom left depicts the latter vessel in Rio de Janeiro showing battle damage. In April 1941 the same ship succeeded in sinking the auxiliary cruiser *Voltaire*. But in May the *Pinguin* fell victim to British cruisers, and in November the *Atlantis* suffered the same fate. The *Kormoran* was stopped by the cruiser *Sydney*, but managed to sink the British ship even though the *Kormoran* herself also had to be abandoned.

In late 1940 the German U-boats, still few in number, were pushed out of the immediate vicinity of the British coast by the aircraft of RAF Coastal Command. As a result it became much more difficult to locate the convoys. After much pressing and persuading, U-boat Command was granted a group of Fw-200 Kondor long-range aircraft to act as spotters, and the type is shown in the picture at the top. In fact, these aircraft seldom directed U-boats to convoys, but they sank many ships themselves. For example it was an Fw-200 which set the 42,348-ton *Empress of Britain* on fire on 26 October (photographed above). It was subsequently sunk by *U 32* before the submarine was sunk in turn by two British destroyers.

The facing page shows the British refrigerated cargo ship *Beacon Grange* breaking up after being torpedoed by *U 552* on 27 April 1941.

(top) German Fw 200 Kondor.

(above) Empress of Britain burning after attack .

(right) MS Beacon Grange sunk by U 552.

On 24 August 1940 the battleship *Bismarck*, displacing 41,700 tons, was commissioned at the Blohm & Voss yard in Hamburg. In the photograph at the top of this page she is seen returning to the yard through the North Sea-Baltic canal for final work after trials in the Baltic. The new heavy cruiser *Prinz Eugen* had also been commissioned in Kiel that same month. The *Bismarck*'s sistership, *Tirpitz*, was due to follow in February 1941. The German Naval Command had great plans for these ships and the two battleships which had entered Brest. The picture above shows the *Bismarck* photographed from the

(top) *Bismarck* returning from trials August 1940.

(above) *Bismarck* at Gotenhafen April 1941

deck of the *Prinz Eugen* in 1941 near Gotenhafen (Gdingen) after further trials.

In Operation Rheinübung the *Scharnhorst* and *Gneisenau* were to make for the Atlantic from Brest, and *Bismarck* and *Prinz Eugen* were to steam from Norway through the Denmark Straits to the same area, where they would await North Atlantic convoys on their regular routes and attack them. The ships were intended to remain at sea for several weeks, and the Germans sent seven tankers, two scout ships and several weather observation ships into the Norwegian Sea and remote regions of the North and mid-Atlantic to keep them supplied.

However, British air attacks on Brest caused such severe damage to the *Scharnhorst* and *Gneisenau* that both had to be withdrawn from the operation. As a result when Operation Rheinübung began on 18 May 1941 only the *Prinz Eugen* put to sea from Kiel and the *Bismarck* from Gotenhafen (Gdingen). In the Kattegat they were reported by the Swedish cruiser *Gotland*, and the British Admiralty immediately learned of this via the Norwegian naval attache in Stockholm. In the meantime, the ships had entered the Grimstad Fjord south of Bergen for refuelling, and there they were discovered by a British Spitfire spotter and photographed from an altitude of 22,000ft. The original photograph is reproduced here at a scale of 1:10,000, orientated to the north.

On 22 May 1941 other British spotter planes found the fjord empty, so the Commander-in-Chief of the Home Fleet, Admiral Tovey, assembled a battle group which included the battlecruiser *Hood* and the new battleship *Prince of Wales* – which still had dockyard workers on board – and sent it out to blockade the Denmark Straits between Iceland and Greenland, at the same time dispatching several cruisers to monitor the Iceland – Shetland narrows. Tovey personally put to sea in his flagship the *King George V*, a sistership to the *Prince of Wales*, together with the carrier *Victorious* and cruisers from Scapa Flow, in order to intercept the German ships.

Aerial photo of *Prinz Eugen* and *Bismarck* in Grimstad Fjord.

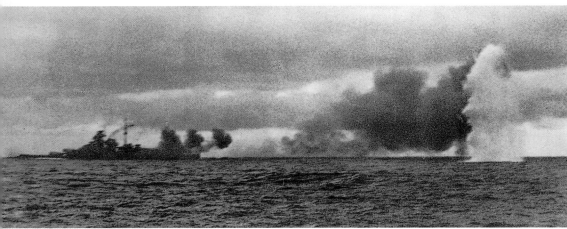

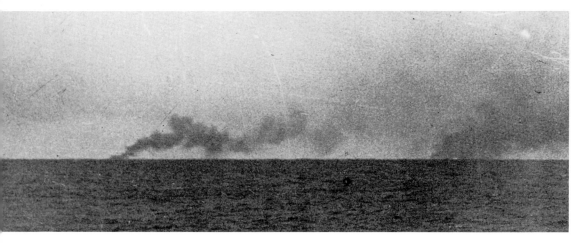

In the picture at top left we see the *Bismarck* steaming to the North in line astern with the *Prinz Eugen*, from which the photograph was taken.

On the evening of 23 May the two heavy cruisers *Norfolk* and *Suffolk*, which had been sent out to patrol the Denmark Straits, sighted *Bismarck* and *Prinz Eugen* and stayed in contact outside the range of the ships' guns. Operating on their report the *Hood*, with Admiral Holland on board, and the *Prince of Wales* came in sight of the German ships at dawn on 24 May. At 0552hrs the *Hood* opened fire on the *Prinz Eugen*. The Germans replied immediately and achieved direct hits on the *Hood* with their first salvos, causing the ship to blow up within five minutes. The second photograph on the left shows *Bismarck* firing at the *Hood*. The *Bismarck* is steaming at high speed, which accounts for the position of the black muzzle smoke from her guns aft of the ship. The white column of water on the right is the impact of a British shell landing short. The third photograph shows the *Prince of Wales* on the left and the burning *Hood* on the right shortly before the explosion. Only three men were rescued from the *Hood*, and Admiral Holland and 1,417 men lost their lives. As the battle continued the *Prince of Wales* was also badly hit by artillery shells, but she was able to get out of range and continue to keep contact, together with the two cruisers. *Bismarck* had received two heavy shell hits and one less severe one, with the result that the ship was leaving an oily wake and her speed was reduced, so the British found it easier to keep contact. The bottom picture shows *Bismarck* firing on the *Prince of Wales* on the evening of 24 May. The ship repeatedly attempted to turn round and thereby force the British ships to turn tail so that the *Prinz Eugen* could disengage, and eventually this plan was successful.

During the bright night of 25 May Admiral Tovey managed to approach close enough to order the launch of Swordfish aircraft from the deck of *Victorious* (picture top right) in order to attack the *Bismarck*. They achieved one torpedo hit which had no effect. During the night the *Bismarck* somehow managed to shake off the British ships keeping contact, though the German Fleet commander Admiral Lütjens, who was on board

(left, from top to bottom)
Bismarck photographed from *Prinz Eugen*.
Bismarck firing on *Hood*.
Prince of Wales (left), *Hood* exploding (right)
Bismarck firing on *Prince of Wales*.

the ship, did not realise this. Thus on the morning of 25 May he sent long radio messages in order to report the results of the battle in the Denmark Straits, and announcing his intention of entering Brest. The British picked up the radio signals and located their source, but the information was incorrectly interpreted on the flagship, with the result that Admiral Tovey's ships, by this time reinforced by other ships withdrawn from convoy duty, fanned out to search – in the wrong direction. It was not until Tovey received a signal from the Admiralty that the error become evident. By this time the *Bismarck* was so far ahead that she could only be intercepted by Force H, steaming up from Gibraltar, and only then if reconnaissance located her. Force H included the battlecruiser *Renown* – far inferior to the *Bismarck* – the carrier *Ark Royal* and the cruiser *Sheffield*.

On the morning of 26 May a Catalina flying boat sighted the *Bismarck*. All the British ships immediately changed course and headed for the new location. In the afternoon a reconnaissance aircraft from *Ark Royal* spotted the *Bismarck*, and soon the *Sheffield* was in contact. In the initial attack the Swordfishes from the *Ark Royal* were forced to take off in severe weather, and they not only failed to hit the *Bismarck* but almost attacked the *Sheffield*. A second attack was made immediately, during which the *Bismarck* was hit by two torpedoes, one of which hit the rudder system and rendered the ship incapable of manoeuvring. In the night four British and one Polish destroyer approached, though none of their torpedoes hit the German ship.

On the morning of 27 May Admiral Tovey's forces were strengthened by the *King George V* and the *Rodney*, which had approached in the meantime. The second picture on the right shows the *King George V* opening fire on the *Bismarck*, which can be seen in the background to the left.

In the third picture the *Rodney* is seen firing off a 16in salvo at the *Bismarck*, and in the bottom photograph, taken from the cruiser *Dorsetshire* at 1031hrs, the burning *Bismarck*, now incapable of fighting, is half-hidden behind the shell plumes of the two British battleships.

(left, from top to bottom)
Swordfish torpedo-planes aboard HMS *Victorious*.
King George V opening fire on *Bismarck*.
Rodney firing 16in salvo at *Bismarck*.
Bismarck on fire, from HMS *Dorsetshire*.

(above) Last photograph of *Bismarck*, taken from *Dorsetshire*.

In the picture above – the last ever taken of the burning *Bismarck* – we see the impact of shells from the British ships to the left of her. At 1035hrs, after she had been hit by two torpedoes from the cruisers *Norfolk* and *Dorsetshire*, the crew fired the explosive charges in the turbine compartment and the *Bismarck* went to the bottom on an even keel.

Pictures of the wreck of the *Bismarck* were taken fifty years later from a deep-diving submersible. The ship lies at a depth of more than 11,000ft, and the photographs show the extent to which all the superstructure and guns of the ship had been destroyed before she sank, and therefore how great must have been the loss of human life before she went down. Even so, a large number of crew members managed to reach the sea with their lifebelts.

The British ships approached the scene to rescue survivors, and the photograph shows seamen from the *Bismarck* swimming in the water before being pulled on board by the crew of the *Dorsetshire* using ropes. The British had to break off the rescue operation when reports of German U-boats were received. In fact, two U-boats had been ordered to meet the *Bismarck* to recover the war diaries, but they arrived too late.

The *Dorsetshire* and the destroyer *Maori* picked up 110 survivors, amongst them only two officers. *U 74* and the weather observation ship *Sachsenwald* later rescued a further five men, but a search by the Spanish cruiser *Canarias* met with no success. Admiral Lütjens, the commander, Kapitän zur See Lindemann, the entire fleet staff and 2,106 crew went down with the *Bismarck*.

A few weeks later the pocket battleship *Lützow* (the former *Deutschland*) received a direct hit by an aerial torpedo in the Skagerrak when putting to sea for an Atlantic operation. By this time the German surface supply ships in the Atlantic had been captured by British hunter groups operating according to the intercepted German radio orders for meeting points, deciphered at Bletchley Park, the first important success of Ultra. It was no longer possible for the Germans to continue the battle against merchant shipping in the Atlantic using heavy ships.

(below) Survivors from *Bismarck* picked up by *Dorsetshire*.

The German Navy used a special version of the army's Enigma code machine to encode their radio signals. Polish cipher experts had penetrated the Enigma system back in 1932, and in 1939 they passed their knowledge to the French and English authorities. It is true that in 1940 the British decoding centre at Bletchley Park had succeeded in breaking the coding methods used by the Luftwaffe, but it had not managed to break the naval key M-3 version by March 1941 in spite of the capture of Enigma code drums. It was not until Bletchley Park had access to the equipment gained in the Lofoten raids (see page 80) that it was possible to decode the day code settings, once the naval version of the encoding machine had been reconstructed. Even then the process was very slow and the delays long. The crucial breakthrough came on 7 May 1941, when the weather observation ship *München* was surprised and her equipment seized, and two days later, when the U-boat *U 110* was forced to surface during a convoy battle and was captured by the boarding party. The two vessels yielded valid coding documents, among them the short signal book and the short weather signal book, and with this information Bletchley Park was able to decode messages classified as 'heimisch' from late May 1941 on, and produce their content without any delay. One direct result was that six of the eight supply vessels sent out to the Atlantic for Operation Rheinübung were intercepted.

For fear that the British breaking of the Enigma process would be deduced, the British Admiralty forbade further targeted actions of this type. But by August 1941 the Bletchley Park experts had gained so much experience that they could crack any day cipher setting with a delay of only three days. Once the day setting had been broken, Bletchley Park was able to send all the day's radio messages to the Submarine Tracking Room by teleprinter using the secrecy level Ultra. This in turn allowed the convoys to be directed around the German U-boat locations.

The photograph below shows the German tanker *Friedrich Breme* in the process of being sunk on 12 June after being hunted down by the cruiser *Sheffield* as a result of an Ultra signal. The photograph was taken from the British cruiser. The capture of the weather ship *Lüneberg* on 28 June yielded the code documents for July.

While *U 570* was searching for the convoy HX.145 in severe weather conditions, following erroneous directions supplied by the German xB-Dienst, the submarine was damaged by a Hudson bomber which had taken off from Iceland. The commander decided to surrender his vessel, and ships were called in to tow the boat to Iceland. Even though the coding machine had been thrown overboard, the boat proved to be an important source of

German tanker *Friedrich Breme* sunk by HMS *Sheffield* after 'Ultra' intercept.

Destroyer *Burwell* taking off crew of captured *U 570*.

technical knowledge to the British, and was eventually re-commissioned as HMS *Graph*. Here the destroyer *Burwell* is closing in on *U 570* in order to take off the crew.

By the second half of 1941 the British convoy control system was so successful that convoys were only attacked if a cruising U-boat accidentally came upon a convoy which had been re-directed. The net result was that around 1,500,000 BRT of convoy shipping reached port safely, which might not have been the case otherwise. U-boat Command did not realise why convoys were no longer being sighted, but to exclude one possible cause attempts were made to improve the security of the coding method, amongst other things. However, it was not until 1 February 1942 that the Germans were able to introduce the new M-4 four rotor ciphering machine, which out-manoeuvred Bletchley Park for 11 months.

On 12 November 1940, just a few days after the re-election of President Roosevelt, the Chief of Naval Operations presented him with four strategic plans. Roosevelt opted for the plan designated Dog, which foresaw the build-up of an offensive capacity in the Atlantic and a defensive capability in the Pacific. This plan became the main theme for the discussions amongst American, British and Canadian staffs which were held in January 1941, and which led to the ABC Staff Agreement concluded on 27 March. This agreement determined the collective Europe-first strategy for any future American involvement in the war. Shortly before this, on 11 March, the American Congress had passed the Lease/lend law, which provided for the supply of war materials on British ships, the repair of damaged warships and the implementation of a large-scale building programme for merchant ships and convoy escort vessels.

On 18 April the security zone to be patrolled by the US Atlantic Fleet was extended to 30° West. Three days later four Task Forces were set up to carry out these patrols, and they were reinforced in May and June by the transfer into the Atlantic of 25 per cent of the Pacific fleet. On 14 June the zone in which battle groups – including battleships, aircraft carriers, cruisers and destroyers – routinely cruised, was extended to 26° West. However, since the Germans had broken off surface ship operations against merchant shipping since the capture of their supply vessels, no serious incidents occurred.

On 9 April 1941 the Americans assumed the protectorate of Greenland, and on 7 July Roosevelt landed a naval brigade in Reykjavik in order to relieve the British garrison stationed there. Now the supply convoys had to be given protection in the German U-boats' operational area. Starting in late July, convoys regularly ran from Newfoundland to Iceland and back, protected by American battle formations. A battle group consisting of battleships, cruisers and destroyers was stationed in Hvalfjord near Reykjavik. Amongst these vessels was the battleship *Mississippi*, shown in the photograph, sailing through heavy seas whilst guarding the Denmark Straits in Autumn 1941.

A sea battle between the Americans and Germans on 5 November 1941 was only averted due to an engine failure on the *Admiral Scheer*.

By February 1941 the US Atlantic Fleet had established a Support Force consisting of three destroyer squadrons and four flying boat squadrons, whose task was to guard

Battleship USS *Mississippi* in the Denmark Strait, autumn 1941.

Destroyer USS Plunkett leading Convoy SC 48.

convoys sailing from Newfoundland around Northern Ireland and into the North Channel, but the force's action was deferred. Radio messages were constantly being decoded by the English and passed on to the Americans, and in June it became clear from this traffic that Hitler wanted at all costs to avoid incidents with American ships while his forces were involved in the German land campaign against the Soviet Union. U-boats reported sighting the US battleship *Texas* in the operational region, but received orders which greatly inhibited their freedom of action.

At the Atlantic conference between Roosevelt and Churchill, which took place between 9 and 12 August 1941, the details of the active involvement in the Battle of the Atlantic by the US Navy – still neutral at this time in the war – were laid down. From 1 September the operational command of convoy traffic West of 26° West passed to the American Chief of Naval Operations, whose commands to the American and Canadian convoy Escort Groups were based partially on the recommendations of the British Admiralty transmitted as Ultra messages (see page 52), while the Admiralty retained its responsibility for the eastern section of the route.

On 4 September the American destroyer *Greer* was directed to the submerged *U 652* by a British aircraft, and the submarine fired torpedoes at the destroyer and missed, after the aircraft had bombed it. This incident gave Roosevelt the excuse to declare his 'shoot on sight order'. From 16 September to 7 December US Task Groups escorted fourteen convoys in each direction, comprising more than 1,200 ships in total. In the foreground of the picture here we see the US destroyer *Plunkett* acting as lead ship of the Canadian – British – French – American escort group guarding the convoy SC.48 in October 1941.

The Mediterranean I
10 June 1940–31 October 1942

Before the armistice of 25 June 1940 the seaworthy French fleet had escaped to ports in North and West Africa. The British feared that the modern battle-worthy ships might fall into German or Italian hands, and at Churchill's insistence the Royal Navy did all they could to prevent this happening. By dint of skilful negotiating in Alexandria Admiral Cunningham succeeded in neutralising the French squadron lying there, but on 3 July Admiral Gensoul refused to accept a British ultimatum presented at Mers-el-Kebir near Oran. At this the British Force H, comprising three battleships, one aircraft carrier, two cruisers and eleven destroyers opened fire on the French ships lying in the harbour. The

picture shows the results of the surprise attack. The old battleship *Bretagne* went up in flames and capsized, the modern *Dunkerque* and the older *Provence* were severely damaged, and the large destroyer *Mogador* lost her stern. Her sistership *Volta* together with two other destroyers and the battleship *Strasbourg* broke through the British ring and escaped to Toulon; 1147 French sailors died. This was a severe blow to the relationship between the formerly allied navies. The French Government in Vichy broke off diplomatic relations with England and sent French aircraft to bomb Gibraltar.

The newly-built French battleship *Riche-*

lieu was at Dakar in its unfinished state, and on 7 July 1940 the British dispatched a fast motor boat carrying an explosive charge as well as torpedo aircraft from the carrier *Hermes*, and the ship was severely damaged in the attack. Two French submarines did not manage to fire at the British ships, but they succeeded in capturing six merchant ships running under a British flag.

The French ships and submarines lying in British ports were occupied by the English, some of them meeting resistance from the crew, although the crews of other vessels joined the Free French navy under General de Gaulle and Admiral Muselier.

The sea war in the Mediterranean was

(left) British attack on French fleet at Mers-el-Kebir.

(above) Italian battleship *Giulio Cesare* firing on HMS *Warspite*.

primarily a struggle for superiority in maritime communications. The aim of the Italian fleet was to secure the convoys carrying troops and materials to supply the army in Libya and Cyrenaica. The British Force H stationed at Gibraltar and the Mediterranean Fleet based in Alexandria had to convoy supplies to the island of Malta, which the Italian Command had failed to conquer at the start of the war. These convoy operations repeatedly resulted in skirmishes and even more serious battles between heavy ships.

On 6 July 1940 an Italian convoy consisting of troop transports left Naples en route for Benghazi, and over a period of time the entire Italian fleet put to sea to guard it after intelligence had reported British cruisers at Malta. The British Mediterranean fleet was also at sea, with the purpose of protecting two Malta convoys. On the morning of 9 July an exchange of fire lasting 105 minutes took place near Punta Stilo between the British flagship *Warspite* and the Italian battleships *Conte di Cavour* and *Giulio Cesare*. The latter ship was badly hit in the engagement, and the Italian fleet commander broke off the action. The picture above was taken from the *Cavour* and shows the *Cesare* in the act of firing. Battles between the cruisers produced no more than a light hit on the Italian cruiser *Bolzano*, and the destroyers' torpedo attacks were unsuccessful, as were those carried out by torpedo aircraft from the British carrier *Eagle*. Attacks by 126 Italian bombers only caused light damage to the cruiser *Gloucester*.

On a voyage to the Italian Dodecanes islands two Italian cruisers were sighted by British spotter aircraft, and on 19 July 1940 they were hunted down near Cape Spada by the Australian cruiser *Sydney* and four destroyers. In the battle which followed the Italian cruiser *Bartolomeo Colleoni* was hit and rendered incapable of manoeuvring (shown above). She was sunk by the torpedoes of destroyers after 525 men had been rescued.

The capture of the submarine *Galilei* in the Red Sea on 19 June and of *Uebi Scebeli* in the Mediterranean on 29 June provided the English with important secret material concerning the operations of the numerous Italian submarines, and this information made a significant contribution to their subsequent lack of success and losses. However, the large British submarines also suffered

serious losses at first.

By August 1940 the Italian fleet boasted an extra two thoroughly modernised battleships as well as two newly built 35,000-ton battleships, and consequently the fleet represented a serious threat to the British supply convoys to Malta and – after the Italian attack against Greece – in the Aegean too. During a Malta operation carried out in the night of 11-12 November, starting from both west and east, the British carrier *Illustrious* sent its Swordfish torpedo aircraft on an aerial attack against the Italian fleet lying in Taranto, in which the battleships *Littorio*, *Caio Duilio* and *Conte di Cavour* (opposite top) sank to the bottom. They were raised, but only the first two were ever returned to service. The Japanese took a keen interest in this attack.

After the Italian battlefleet's fighting power had been halved by this action, the British were confident enough to send a convoy through the Mediterranean from Gibraltar to Alexandria and at the same time to bring two convoys to Malta and into the Aegean from the east. When an aircraft reported a sighting of the British formation in the Western Mediterranean the Italian fleet commander put to sea with two battleships, six cruisers and fourteen destroyers in an effort to intercept them. On 27 November 1940 the Italians indeed encountered British ships, but it was Force D pushing forward to join the convoy the south of Sardinia rather than Force H, and they broke off the battle after a brief exchange of fire in which the British cruisers *Manchester* and *Sheffield* took part, shown in the photograph opposite.

(left) Italian cruiser *Bartolomeo Colleoni* crippled by Australian cruiser *Sydney* and four destroyers.

(below) Italian battleship *Conte di Cavour* sunk by air attack at Taranto.

(bottom) British cruisers *Manchester* and *Sheffield* off Sardinia.

The setback caused by the Greek counter-offensive in Albania in November 1940 and the start of a successful British counter-offensive in Cyrenaica in December caused Hitler to send the X flying corps to Sicily. During a renewed British operation on 10 and 11 January 1941 aimed at bringing convoys through the Mediterranean to Malta and Piraeus, German Ju-87 dive bombers attacked British units for the first time, sinking the cruiser *Southampton* and achieving six serious hits on the carrier *Illustrious*, whose burning flight deck is shown in the picture on the left. The carrier was brought in to Malta where it was struck by several more bombs in further attacks, but in late January she escaped to Alexandria and thence to the Norfolk Navy Yard in the USA for repairs.

(left) Bomb damage to British carrier *Illustrious*.

(below) Italian battleship *Vittorio Veneto* after torpedo hit.

Greek battleships *Kilkis* and *Lemnos* sunk by German air attack in Piraeus.

After an erroneous report from the German Luftwaffe about successful torpedo strikes on heavy units of the British Mediterranean fleet, the Italian fleet put to sea on 26 March 1941 under German pressure in order to capture British convoys bound for the Aegean. Bletchley Park had decoded two Italian and German radio messages concerning an Italian operation in the Crete region, and thus warned the British Mediterranean fleet left Alexandria and put to sea. After a futile battle with a British cruiser formation coming from the Aegean and a failed attack by torpedo aircraft from the British carrier *Formidable*, the Italian fleet ommander broke off the operation. In a second attack British torpedo aircraft achieved one hit each on the battleship *Vittorio Veneto* and the cruiser *Pola*, which was rendered incapable of manoeuvring. The same night the *Pola*

was sunk by the British battleships which had approached in the meantime, together with the two cruisers *Fiume* and *Zara* which had been sent to help, and two destroyers. All the Italian ships were sunk near Cape Matapan. The *Vittorio Veneto* was damaged by a torpedo but escaped, as shown in the photograph on the opposite page.

A few days later, on 6 April 1941, the German attack against Yugoslavia and Greece began. While the German troops forced the Yugoslavian and Greek armies to surrender, the German X flying corps attacked Piraeus repeatedly on 7 April and again from 21 to 24 April, sinking numerous merchant ships and the old battleships *Kilkis* and *Lemnos*, which are shown in the centre and background of the photograph here. The British had to evacuate their troops which had been transported to Greece. 50,672 men

were taken on board ship, but 223,000 Greeks and 21,900 British were captured. On 20 May the Germans started their attack on Crete with aerial landings. British cruisers and destroyers attempting to attack formations of motor-gliders carrying mountain troops were partly frustrated by the intervention of two Italian torpedo boats. On 27 May the British Mediterranean fleet began the task of evacuating the island under constant German air attack. Three cruisers and six destroyers were sunk, while three battleships, one aircraft carrier, six cruisers and five destroyers were damaged, and 2,011 British seamen died. Of the 42,640 defenders some 17,000 reached Egypt. The German casualties amounted to 6,580 dead, wounded and missing.

(top) British battleships *Malaya* and *Ramilles* and cruiser *Kent* photographed from *Warspite*.

(above) Italian and German freighters making for Tripoli.

In an attempt to disrupt supplies for an Italian offensive against Egypt, the British battleships *Warspite*, *Malaya* and *Ramillies* and the cruiser *Kent* bombarded the Italian ports of Bardia and Capuzzo. The photograph at the top on the opposite page, taken from the *Warspite*, shows the three other British ships on the approach.

In view of the incipient catastrophe in Cyrenaica – 140,000 Italians were taken prisoner during the British offensive – in January 1941 the German Command decided to dispatch troops to Africa under Lieutenant-General Rommel. On 11 February the first convoy arrived at Tripoli consisting of three freighters guarded by four Italian destroyers and torpedo boats. Other convoys followed, and by late March Rommel was able to initiate a surprise thrust which regained Cyrenaica in April, although he was unable to capture Tobruk whose seaborne supply line was secured by the English.

These convoys, consisting primarily of Italian freighters with a few German vessels carrying war materials, tankers for fuel and passenger steamers for the troops, and guarded by Italian destroyers and torpedo boats, were the lifeline for the German-Italian army in Africa. The lower photograph on the left shows freighters under escort en route to Tripoli.

In June 1941 the English succeeded in breaking into the radio traffic between the Italian command stations in Rome and Tripoli, which was encoded using the Hagelin C38m machine. As a result, the British submarines and aircraft stationed at Malta received accurate information on the location and timing of convoys, and were able to make their attacks more and more accurate. September saw a significant success: on 15 September decoded Ultra messages had supplied information on a troop transport convoy which included the large Italian passenger steamers *Vulcania*, *Oceania* and *Neptunia*, with a guard consisting of five destroyers. Four submarines were sent to attack the convoy, and *Upholder* sank the *Oceania* and *Neptunia*. The destroyers were able to rescue 6,500 shipwrecked sailors who were swimming in the water, but 384 died (see the photograph below).

In March 1941 the losses incurred by forty-five Italian convoys, comprising a total tonnage of more than 670,000grt, were only 1.1 per cent, but the rate of loss rose in September to 24.3 per cent although there were only twenty-eight convoys of 330,000grt. In December the figure rose to 30 per cent despite a further decline in the number of convoys (twenty-two), amounting to only 120,000grt. Fuel supplies were the primary responsibility of Germany, and fuel shortages often prevented the large Italian ships carrying out convoy guard duty against British cruisers stationed at Malta. In any case the British ships' radar apparatus gave them the advantage in night battles. Faced with this desperate supply situation Rommel's only course was to withdraw before the British offensive took place.

Survivors from *Oceania* and *Neptunia* being rescued.

In November 1941 the crisis in North Africa forced the Axis powers to re-double their efforts: there were six German U-boats already in the Mediterranean, and now a further sixteen were ordered to join them after first passing through the Straits of Gibraltar. This they did in mid-November. Almost immediately – on 13 November – *U 81* succeeded in torpedoing the carrier *Ark Royal* as she returned to Gibraltar from an operation, and the ship had to be abandoned the following day (photograph left). On 25 November *U 331* broke through the escort of

(top left) HMS *Ark Royal* hit by torpedo from *U 81*.

(below left) Battleship HMS *Barham* exploding.

(below) Cruiser HMS *Penelope*.

the British Mediterranean Fleet which had put to sea to attack convoys, and hit the battleship *Barham* with three torpedoes, tearing the ship asunder in a single gigantic explosion. The lower photograph captures precisely this moment of annihilation, probably as no other comparable catastrophe has been recorded. On 19 December three Italian *Maiali* (human torpedoes) which had been launched from the submarine *Scire* managed to enter the harbour of Alexandria and laid limpet mines under the battleships *Queen Elizabeth* and *Valiant*, which were sent to the bottom in shallow water. On the same day the British Force K, consisting of three cruisers and four destroyers, strayed into an Italian minefield when on an operation from Malta aimed at intercepting a convoy off

Tripoli. The cruiser *Neptune* and the destroyer *Kandahar* sank with the loss of around 550 men, while the cruisers *Aurora* and *Penelope* were damaged. The picture below shows the *Penelope* after arriving at Malta, her hull side pocked with bomb splinter marks.

The loss of these heavy British units made it possible for the Italian fleet to bring a number of large convoys to North Africa once more. This in turn gave Rommel the means to start a new attack. The action began on 21 January 1942 and reached El Gazala. In April continual aerial attacks by the German 2nd Air Fleet against Malta forced the British to withdraw their surface ships, submarines and bombers from Malta to Egypt.

The heavy air attacks on Malta caused the British fighter formations to reduce their operation more and more. Rommel's thrust into El Gazala prevented the British based in Cyrenaica guarding their convoys coming from the East. As a result the Gibraltar-based Force H, consisting of the carriers *Eagle* and *Argus* and on two occasions the USS *Wasp*, pushed forward into the region to the South of Sardinia, so that they could fly Spitfire fighter aircraft in to Malta.

In June 1942 it was decided to break through to Malta from west and east with the

(top left) Malta convoy escorts making smoke.

(below left) British aircraft carriers *Indomitable*, *Victorious* and *Eagle* escorting Convoy 'Pedestal'.

(below) Tanker *Ohio* reaches Malta.

help of forces of the Home Fleet, running convoys of six and eleven transports respectively. The picture on the left shows escort vessels of one these convoys making smoke. The convoy Harpoon lost one transport south of Sardinia after an attack by Italian aircraft. The convoy guard force had to withstand battles with two Italian cruisers and four destroyers off Cape Bon, in which the British destroyer *Bedouin* (the forward ship in the photograph at top left) was sunk. Stuka attacks sank three transports, and off Malta the remainder of the convoy strayed into a mine barrage. The convoy Vigorous lost two ships, one cruiser and three destroyers as a result of air attacks, S-boats and submarines, and was eventually called back since by that time the Italian fleet had put to sea from Taranto.

After this failure – only two ships made it

as far as Malta – no new attempt could be undertaken until August, when the PQ.17 operation in the Arctic had been completed (see page 82). The three aircraft carriers *Eagle*, *Victorious* and *Indomitable* were to supply the aerial escort (as shown in the photograph at bottom left) and a cruiser formation was intended to push through the convoy Pedestal consisting of fourteen transports. However, German and Italian aircraft, submarines and S-boats sank the *Eagle*, two cruisers, nine transports and one destroyer, while the *Indomitable* and two cruisers were severely damaged. Only four transports and the tanker *Ohio* reached Malta, the latter severely damaged and shown in the photograph below, taken in the island's harbour.

While Malta was having difficulty defending itself and had no attack forces available, the German-Italian supply line to Africa was able to operate relatively unhindered until the late Summer of 1942. After Rommel's offensive, which led to the fall of Tobruk on 21 June and took the Germans as far as El Alamein on 30 June, German-Italian convoys were able to run from Sicily along the Tunisian coast to Tripoli, from the Ionian sea to Benghasi, and even from Piraeus and Crete to Tobruk. The photograph here shows a convoy gathering in a Cretan harbour, while a netlayer in the foreground lays a net blockade to ward off submarines. The Aegean convoys running from here under the leadership of the German Admiral

received their operational directions in writing before they put to sea, and the tactical decisions of the leader of the escort ships were left up to him. This system largely eliminated the radio traffic which could have given the English the chance to decode and interpret the messages. It was a different matter with the convoys which were directed strictly from Rome, with their route plans broadcast by radio. The evacuation of the British attack forces from Malta denied the English the use of the Ultra radio decoding system for effective attacks in the period from April to September 1942.

After the remnants of the British Pedestal convoy had arrived at Malta in August, further supplies reached the island

Convoy gathering in a harbour on Crete, with anti-submarine net being laid from netlayer in foreground.

in September, in particular supplies of fighter aircraft. These events, together with the return of the 10th British submarine flotilla with its manoeuvrable U-class boats, represented the turning of the tide. German and Italian losses started to rise again until October and, particularly, November 1942, when they reached dramatic levels.

In the meantime the British 8th Army in Egypt had been reinforced with fresh troops, new tanks and materials by means of extremely circuitous voyages around Africa. Rommel had to cope with this change of events at a time when he was faced with an increasingly difficult supply situation. On 23 October 1942 a barrage by British artillery marked the start of the 8th Army's attack on El Alamein, before which the German Army in Africa, its supplies exhausted, was forced to retreat. The largely destroyed harbour of Tobruk (shown in the picture below on 16 October, still with German convoy ships in it), which had been held from 1940 to 1942 by Australian, British and South African formations, once again fell into the hands of the Allies on 13 November 1942, but Rommel escaped the pursuit and reached Tripoli.

German ships at Tobruk.

The Baltic
22 June 1941– 31 August 1944

During the German offensives in the north and west of Europe the Soviet Union conquered from Finland Karelia and the base of Hango in the Winter War, and in June and July 1940 annexed the three Baltic republics. On 31 July Hitler declared to the Armed Forces chiefs his decision 'to defeat the Soviet Union in a five-month campaign in the Spring of 1941'.

In the overall plan the army, supported by the Luftwaffe, was to carry out fast troop thrusts, some of them into the Baltic region and in the direction of Leningrad. The navy wanted to tie down the Soviet Baltic fleet by laying massive mine barrages in the central Baltic and the Bay of Finland. In contrast, the 'Baltic runway' was only to be used for troop transport to Finland, which linked up with the German plans in the 'continuation war'. On 14 June 1941 German troops embarked at Stettin for Finland, depicted here on the left.

Even before the Germans attacked the Soviet Union on 22 June 1941 the German-Finnish mine barrages were laid as planned. On the night of 23 June the Soviet Baltic fleet began laying its own mine barrages, but the cover group ran into the Apolda barrage. One destroyer sank, but the cruiser *Maxim Gorkiy* and a destroyer were brought back, albeit severely damaged. Less lucky were three German minelayers which ran into a Swedish mine barrage near Øland on 9 July and sank. These mines had been laid at the request of the Germans. The minelayers were the *Tannenberg* (seen in the foreground in the photograph opposite top), the *Preussen* (burning in the background) and the *Hansestadt Danzig*.

German U-boats and S-boats accounted for the loss of several Soviet submarines and smaller vessels. In the photograph on the right rescued Russian prisoners, some of them wounded, lie on the deck of a German S-boat.

(left) German troops embarking for Finland.

(top right) German minelayers *Tannenberg*, *Preussen* and *Hansestadt Danzig*, mined July 1941.

(below right) Russian prisoners on German S-boat.

On 8 August 1941 the first sections of the German 18th Army reached the coast of the Bay of Finland and thereby cut off the Soviet troops fighting in Estland and still stationed on Oesel and Dagoe. Supplying these troops now became the main task of the Soviet Baltic fleet. Ju-88s of the coastal Fliegergruppe 806 were put into action to halt these transports, and on 8 August they sank the destroyer *Karl Marx* in Loksa Bay, shown top left.

On the same day German and Finnish minelayers began laying the Juminda mine barrages. Soviet ships continued to run supply ships to the Soviet X Corps, by this time squeezed into an ever contracting region around Reval, and five minehunters and several transports were sunk by mines before the order was given to evacuate Reval on 27 August. Of the 153 Soviet warships and merchant ships which took part in this operation foty-two were lost to aerial attacks and mines, amongst them eighteen of the twenty-one transports. However, the small vessels which made up the majority of the ships rescued 12,160 men from sinking ships, while about 6,000 reached Kronstadt on the ships themselves.

The evacuation of Hangös lasted from October to December, in which time twenty-five of the eighty-eight ships employed sank due to mines, taking around 4,000 men with them. Twenty-three thousand men reached Kronstadt. When the transport *Iosef Stalin* ran onto four mines, minehunters managed to rescue 650 men but were forced to abandon the ship herself. The vessel, carrying 2,000 men and many dead (pictured bottom left) was eventually towed in by German patrol boats on 3 December.

In September German and Finnish troops surrounded Leningrad, and after this time supplies could only be brought to the city by the laborious route over the Ladoga lake – in winter over the ice. The defenders of Leningrad were supported by the guns of battleships, cruisers and destroyers and also naval brigades formed from ships' crews. In the photograph above a Soviet captain, 3rd rank, is standing next to an AA position on a bridge over the Neva. In an attempt to shut down the ships' artillery, Stukas carried out an attack from 21 to 24 September, hitting the battleships *Marat* and *Oktyabrskaya Revoluciya* (picture bottom right, off Kronstadt), and causing severe damage to other ships

(top left) Soviet destroyer *Karl Marx*
(bottom left) Transport *Iosef Stalin* under tow.
(top right) Soviet position on the Neva bridge.
(bottom right) Battleship *Marat* hit.

German victims of mines: (top) freighter sunk by submarine-laid mine; (bottom) steamer
Gneisenau sunk by British air-laid mine.

After the ice had broken up in the spring of 1942 new German-Finnish mine barrages were laid in the east and west sections of the Bay of Finland, but these measures were not sufficient to prevent Soviet submarines breaking out into the Baltic. There they sank twenty ships, amongst them several Swedish vessels, and damaged a further eight. Other ships sank on Soviet submarine-laid mines. In 1943 the Germans laid a net barrier which prevented further breakouts until Autumn 1944.

A serious problem for the Germans was the mine offensive carried out by British aircraft in 1942, and again more intensively in 1943. The aircraft often succeeded in blocking the remaining swept passages as the minesweepers did their essential work, and the mines themselves caused increasing losses. The top picture here shows a freighter sunk by a Soviet submarine mine off Swinemünde in August 1942, while the picture below is of the German passenger steamer *Gneisenau* which struck an aerial mine off Gjedser on 2 May 1943.

The Black Sea

22 June 1941–31 August 1944

When the German and Romanian armies carried out their attack on the Ukraine they could not expect any support from the sea since the Soviet Black Sea fleet held absolute control in that area. However, as early as August 1941 the Soviet navy was forced to concentrate on supplying the besieged port of Odessa, and in October ships had to evacuate the city. Initially, they carried away a large proportion of the inhabitants, but on 15 and 16 October they evacuated 35,000

defenders in a successful operation. At the same time the German siege of the fortress of Sevastopol began. The Black Sea Fleet now had to harness all its forces to give artillery support to the defenders of Sevastopol, to bring in reinforcements and to evacuate wounded men. In December the fleet carried out a a major landing operation involving large numbers of soldiers at the port of Feodosiya and on the north and east coasts of the Kerch peninsula, in an effort

both to cut off the German troops stationed there and to break through the siege ring around Sevastopol from the rear. The Germans were forced to abandon Kerch, but they managed to avoid the threatened envelopment and hold a blockade position. In the bitter fighting both sides suffered great losses. The photograph here shows inhabitants of the Kerch peninsula after its re-conquest, searching amongst the dead for members of their families.

Soviet submarines were employed to disrupt the traffic around the Romanian and Bulgarian coastlines, but they met an obstacle in the form of mines laid there, and suffered considerable losses.

Searching the battlefield on the Kerch peninsula.

After the evacuation of Nikolayev and its great dockyards on 16 August 1941 and the surrounding of Sevastopol at the end of October, the Soviet Black Sea Fleet had lost its main bases. From that time on it had to operate from the inadequately equipped Caucasus ports. Many ships were lying at Sevastopol awaiting repair to battle damage, but not all of them could be towed away in time. During Stuka attacks by the IV Fliegerkorps in November the cruiser *Chervona Ukraina* was severely damaged and sank. The same fate awaited the destroyer *Bystryi* which had been sunk in June after hitting a mine, but had been raised, and also the new vessel *Sovershennyi* seen above. However, all the serviceable Soviet ships, from the battleship to destroyers and even submarines, together with the few fast transports, continued their voyages between the Caucasus ports and Sebastopol, bringing fresh troops, bombarding German positions and returning with the wounded.

By May 1942 the German 11th Army had destroyed the three armies of the Soviet

Crimean front on the Kerch peninsula, and on 7 June it set off to attack Sebastopol, supported by very heavy artillery and the Luftwaffe. The city had been under siege for more than seven months. Completing anything from two to six voyages the cruiser *Molotov*, six destroyers and two transports brought more than 10,000 new Soviet troops into the fortification and evacuated many wounded men. During this action the two transports and three of the destroyers were sunk. In a final effort on 27 June the destroyer *Tashkent* embarked a further 2,300 wounded soldiers and civilians. Numerous near-misses by bombs caused damage beneath the water line and 1,900 tons of water entered the ship, itself displacing only 3,200 tons. After rescuing 1,975 persons the ship just reached Novorossiysk before sinking and grounding on the bottom. The hulk was finally destroyed by bombs on 2 July. The photograph at the bottom of the facing page shows the wreck of the *Tashkent* after German troops had occupied the port on 9 September.

(above) Soviet destroyer *Sovershennyi* sunk by Stukas at Sevastopol, October 1941.

(top right) Romanian troops landing on the Taman Peninsula.

(bottom right) Wreck of the *Tashkent*.

By that time the German 46th Infantry Division and the Romanian 3rd Infantry Division stationed on Kerch had landed on the Taman peninsula, with the aim of providing support to the German formations pushing forward to the Caucasus from the north. In the picture at the top on the right Romanian troops are being landed by inflatable boat from the German Siebel ferries in the background.

However, the Soviets succeeded in halting the German attack at Novorossiysk and carried out their own landings, making use of the last available ships of the Black Sea Fleet which were brought out of reserve from the Trans-Caucasus. The Germans were never able to penetrate past this point on the Black Sea coast.

(above) German evacuation of Odessa.

(left) Minesweeper *Iskatel* in the Black Sea.

When the German 6th Army was surrounded at Stalingrad in the late Autumn of 1942 the tide also began to turn in the Black Sea. Soviet submarines pushed out as far as the Romanian Black Sea coast and the Crimea, followed by surface ships such as the minesweeper *Iskatel*, shown in the picture on the left. There they tried to intercept the German-Romanian supply convoys. In one such operation, on 6 October 1943, three of the seven Soviet destroyers still serviceable were sunk by German Stuka attacks, and this prompted Stalin to stop the further use of surface ships for this purpose, as the remaining units were needed as training ships prior to the resumption of a large-scale fleet building programme due to start in late 1944.

Early in 1944 the Red Army offensives reached the Dnyestr. Threatened by encirclement, the Germans evacuated 9,300 wounded, 14,845 soldiers and 54,000 tons of material from Odessa using ferry barges and small vessels. The picture on the left, taken on 8 April from a boat of the 3rd Landing-craft flotilla, gives an impression of the event. After the Soviet breakthrough into the Crimea Sevastopol could not be expected to hold out for long. In spite of Hitler's refusal to initiate the evacuation in good time, over 150,000 German and Romanian soldiers were evacuated by sea and air, while 8,100 died on board ships which were sunk by aircraft, motor-torpedo boats and submarines. 78,000 were left behind, dead or captured. In the photograph on the right Soviet naval infantrymen are seen storming Sevastopol, and in the picture below overloaded ferry barges arrive at Constanza carrying evacuated German soldiers.

(right) Soviet naval infantry attacking Sevastopol.

(below) Evacuated German troops at Constanza.

The Arctic and Norway

22 June 1941–8 May 1945

Churchill considered it important to pose a threat to Norway and thereby tie up powerful German forces. An initial raid against the Lofotens was carried out on 3 and 4 March 1941, in which seven German convoy transports were sunk. At the same time the patrol boat *Krebs* was damaged and rendered incapable of manoeuvring, and a boarding party from the destroyer *Somali* took from it secret material which enabled the English to crack the naval Enigma cipher 'Home Waters' (see page 52). The picture above was taken from on board the *Somali* and shows Svolvaer on the Lofotens with its fish processing installations in flames after bombardment.

Hitler's fear of a threat to Norway, made more acute by a renewed raid in December 1941, forced him to move heavy ships to the area. In the autumn of 1941, after the start of the German attack on the Soviet Union, the Germans realised that the British had begun to send convoys carrying supplies from Iceland to Arkhangelsk and Murmansk via the North Sea. The German Naval Command saw promising possibilities here for surface ships. From January to March 1942 all available heavy ships were transferred to Norway, the number of U-boats was increased and the Luftwaffe force was strengthened. From 5 to 13 March U-boats, four destroyers along with the *Tirpitz* attempted to locate British convoys. Forewarned by Ultra radio deciphering the

British were able to evade them, and the British cover groups avoided *Tirpitz* with the exception of one failed carrier air attack. During the next German push against a convoy with a force of three destroyers on 29 March *Z 26* was hit by the British cruiser *Trinidad* in driving snow, and was severely damaged. Eighty-eight men of the crew were rescued by *Z 24* and *Z 25* before the ship was abandoned, and the remaining 243 men lost their lives. The photograph on the right shows the burning ship in the throws of sinking.

(above) Fisheries installations burning at Svolvaer.

(right) German destroyer Z 26 sinking after attack by HMS *Trinidad*, 29/3/41.

(above) Tanker in Convoy PQ 18 explodes after U-boat attack.

(below right) HMS *Trinidad* sunk by air attack.

By this time the German Luftwaffe in northern Norway had been strengthened with the addition of Ju-88 bombers and He-111 torpedo aircraft belonging to KG.26 and KG.30. An operation against the convoy pair PQ.14 and QP.10 from 11 to 17 April 1942 ended with the sinking of two ships by German aircraft and two more by U-boats, though the three destroyers which had put to sea failed to find any targets. Stuka attacks against Murmansk caused further damage.

The next convoy heading west from Murmansk was QP.11, accompanied by the cruiser *Edinburgh*. The ship was torpedoed by *U 456* on 30 April. Three German destroyers had been sent out to attack the convoy but they were not able to fight off the close escort and sank only one ship. The destroyers then happened upon the damaged *Edinburgh*. In a violent battle in snow showers *Z 24* and *Z 25* torpedoed the cruiser and caused severe damage to two destroyers with

their guns, but the leading boat, *Hermann Schoemann* was hit by the mortally wounded *Edinburgh* and had to be abandoned, as did the cruiser. German aircraft sank three ships from PQ.15. The cruiser *Trinidad*, escorting PQ.13, was hit by her own torpedo which had taken up a circular course as a result of icing. She reached Murmansk and the damage was repaired temporarily, but on the return voyage she was sunk by Ju-88s of KG.30 on 14 May. She is seen sinking in the photograph on the opposite page.

Whilst the convoy QP.12 came through unhindered at the end of May, PQ.16 was not so fortunate. The convoy was directed round a U-boat formation thanks to an Ultra radio decrypt, but on 26 and 27 May seven freighters were sunk by aerial attacks, and 147 tanks, 77 aircraft and 770 vehicles were also lost.

The next convoy, PQ.17, had been postponed from June 1942 to early July on

account of a Malta convoy. This time all available German surface ships were to be employed against it in addition to U-boats and aircraft. The convoy was to be covered by the Home Fleet, backed up between Iceland and Bear Island by a US battle formation which included several cruisers and a battleship-carrier group, in addition to its submarine guard. From Sweden the British Admiralty learned of the intentions of the Germans, and this prompted the First Sealord, on the evening of 4 July, to order the convoy to be broken up and dispersed. The results of this decision were disastrous: German U-boats and aircraft sank twenty-four of the thirty-six ships carrying 430 tanks, 210 aircraft, 3,350 vehicles and 99,316 tons of material, while the German surface ships were called back.

(above) German BV 138 flying-boat refuelling from *U 255*, 1943.

(left) Near miss on *Admiral Scheer*.

The convoy PQ.18 was also delayed by a Malta convoy, and was not able to run until September. The escorts consisted of an escort carrier with sixteen fleet destroyers. Nevertheless the convoy lost ten ships to U-boats and aircraft and the photograph above shows the convoy on 14 September just as a tanker is hit.

The postponement of the convoy PQ.18 in August 1942 resulted in the German Command carrying out an operation with the *Admiral Scheer* and two U-boats in the Kara Sea, where their task was to intercept Soviet convoys on the northeast passage. However, the ice formations prevented the *Scheer* from approaching the convoy after it had been spotted by the ship's aircraft, and the Germans had to be satisfied with sinking the ice-breaker *Sibiryakov* after the ship put up brave opposition. The picture on the left shows the impact of a shell from the ice-breaker close to the *Scheer*. The *Scheer*

attacked the base of Dikson on 27 August and caused damage to land installations, one large guardship and two steamers.

During a repeat operation carried out by the *Lützow* in 1943 the U-boat *U 255* refuelled a BV-138 flying boat on the east coast of Novaya Semlya (pictured above). However, four flights extending to the Vilkitskii Straits failed to detect any targets which would have justified the use of the *Lützow*. As a result it remained the business of the U-boats to sink ships on the Siberian sea route with torpedoes and mines in 1943 and 1944.

In September 1943 the *Tirpitz* and the *Scharnhorst* led a raid against Spitzbergen with nine destroyers. While the *Scharnhorst* group destroyed the installations in the Grønfjord and Advent Bay, the *Tirpitz* bombarded Barentsburg and set the town alight, depicted in the photograph at the top of the opposite page taken from the deck of the battleship.

In an attempt to gain information about future weather developments, German U-boats set up automatic weather stations on islands in the Arctic and on Labrador. Long-range aircraft also flew weather reconnaissance and trawlers converted into weather observation ships were dispatched to the pack ice on the eastern coast of Greenland. The last ship of this type, the *Externsteines*, was forced to surrender to two icebreakers of the US Coast Guard on 16 October 1944 (shown below).

(right) *Tirpitz* bombarding Barentsburg, September 1943.

(below) German *Externsteine* surrendering to US coastguard off Greenland.

On New Year's Eve 1942/43 an attempted attack on the convoy JW.51B by the cruisers *Admiral Hipper* and *Lützow* with six destroyers failed due to skilful defence on the part of the British. Hitler replaced Raeder with Dönitz, who dissuaded Hitler from his plan to decommission the heavy German ships. For the summer of 1943 the British Admiralty had been forced to break off the convoy traffic to Murmansk on account of the situation in the Atlantic. Before the convoys were resumed the Admiralty decided to attempt to eliminate the heavy German ships with a mini-submarine attack, but only the *Tirpitz*, lying in Altafjord, was damaged. When German spotter aircraft and U-boats reported sighting the convoy JW.55B in late December 1943, the *Scharnhorst* and five destroyers put to sea to take up the attack.

(left) Destroyer HMS *Saumarez* off the Kola fjord.

(bottom left) Survivors from *Scharnhorst*.

(right) Beaufighters of RAF Coastal Command attacking German convoy with rockets.

In the stormy weather of the polar night three British cruisers kept the heavy German ship at a safe distance and directed the battleship *Duke of York* towards her. On 26 December the latter's radar-guided artillery and torpedoes from the destroyers sank the *Scharnhorst*. In the picture on the left we see the participating destroyer *Saumarez* off the Kola fjord, while in the photograph below the thirty-six survivors rescued from the *Scharnhorst* are seen entering an English port after being taken prisoner. 1,803 of their comrades drowned in the Polar Sea on Boxing Day 1943.

In the Autumn of 1943 aerial attacks by the RAF against the German convoy traffic along the Norwegian west coast were intensified. They were carried out by aircraft of RAF Coastal Command based in Scotland and the Shetlands. In October aircraft from the American carrier *Ranger*, on loan to the Home Fleet, carried out the first massive attack against the shipping off the Westfjord, which was out of range of Coastal Command's aircraft. The air force of the Soviet North Fleet had been reinforced by supplies of modern aircraft under the Lend-Lease agreement, and now attacked the convoys off the polar coast with increasing ferocity. The German fighter aircraft forces in Norway were too weak to provide adequate protection to all convoys in addition to guarding the fleet, and the result was a steady rise in total losses and a steady fall in transport capacity. In the picture above Beaufighters of RAF Coastal Command attack an German convoy escort vessel off the Norwegian west coast with rockets.

The Norwegian coast, which extends for a distance of about 2,000 nautical miles from Oslo to Kirkenes, was vital to the Germans. On the one hand it formed the main supply route for the German mountain troops stationed on the Lapland front, for the aircraft groups, and the fleet units and U-boats stationed in northern Norway. It was also the route by which Swedish ore was transported from Narvik to Germany when Botten Bay was frozen up during the winter. The Polar Sea road ran from Oslo to Kirkenes through the Norwegian mountains and around the deeply indented fjords, and its 2,527km length had been completed under the greatest difficulty and hardship, but neither this route nor the roads through northern Finland had sufficient capacity to replace the sea route. The fissured mountain coast with its innumerable inshore rock islands and fjords offered many hiding places for shipping, with AA batteries for protection, where the German convoys, which could only travel at night, sought shelter by day. The photograph here shows a typical scene.

Wherever the sea route could not be directed inside the offshore islands, the convoys were protected by mine barriers, laid where the depth of water allowed.

Off southwestern and western Norway the main danger was from the British submarines and a few Free French, Dutch and Norwegian submarines, most of which carried out their first enemy actions here after commissioning. In 1942 occasional attacks were carried out by Norwegian motor torpedo boats operating from the Shetlands, and often hiding behind islands or in fjords. After the autumn 1943 the Allied air attacks became increasingly dangerous. The use of these forces was supported by British Ultra radio decrypting, since German radio traffic employed the Heimisch or Hydra which the British were able to decipher.

Off northern Norway the main threat to German shipping was from torpedo and mine attacks by Soviet submarines, but the submarine commanders were usually over-optimistic in their reports of success, as a good number of their torpedoes often detonated

German convoy in a Norwegian fjord waiting for nightfall.

on rocks behind the ships they had in their sights. For example, in 1943 about one hundred U-boat contacts and attacks were reported, but only ten ships and eight convoy vessels were lost, which corresponded to 0.7 per cent of the 6,300,000grt shipping capacity of the convoys concerned.

In 1944 the Soviets carried out combined operations. Secret agents or aerial reconnaissance reported the convoys, and submarines waiting outside the German mine barrages off the promontories, would attack them. Off the Varanger peninsula attack aircraft, torpedo aircraft and motor-torpedoe boats were also used. Even so, the losses hardly exceeded 1 per cent of the total capacity of the convoy ships.

To guard German convoy traffic, destroyers were usually only available when they were transferring to different areas. The most effective guard ships were the Type 35 and Type 40 minesweeping boats, and three newly-built gunboats which had previously belonged to the Dutch. However, the main burden was borne by the fishing vessels and whalers which had been fitted out as patrol boats and U-boat hunters. As an example the photograph below shows the submarine hunter *UJ 1709* (the ex fishing vessel *Westpreussen*) lying at anchor with a convoy in July 1944 in the South Norwegian Fede-Fjord.

Initially these boats only carried relatively light armament. For example, on 3 December 1941 the large Soviet submarine *K 3* surfaced off Rolvsoy after an abortive torpedo attack, sank the submarine hunter *UJ 1708* with its two 4in cannon and then

escaped. As the aerial threat became ever graver, the patrol boats and submarine hunters were fitted with one 4in or 3.5in gun and 37mm and 20mm AA guns in single, twin or quad mounts on raised platforms. Their submarine hunter armament consisted of depth charge launchers and roll-off depth charge rails at the stern, but in most cases the submarine hunters only carried ultrasound locating apparatus.

Fishing steamers converted into auxiliary minesweepers and, at a later period, proper minesweeping boats, were employed to ward off the danger of Soviet submarines on the polar coast and the mine blockades which were laid repeatedly along the west

coast by the Free-French submarine *Rubis* (the most successful minelaying submarine of the entire war). It was a mine barrage which was laid by *Rubis* in the Feiestein Channel off Stavanger in September 1944 that sank two large freighters totalling 11,044grt, together with two German escort vessels. Almost two hundred seamen lost their lives in this incident.

From 1940 to the start of 1945 a total of 30.4 million grt of convoy shipping capacity travelled along the Norway route, and of this only 0.5 per cent was lost; and of that the majority was not lost until the final year of the war.

German *UJ1709* in Fede fjord.

From August 1944 to May 1945 eight strong-ly-protected Allied Murmansk convoys steamed in both directions. Of their 442 ships only eight were lost, but the German U-boats also torpedoed and sank twelve escort vessels. The Liberty ship shown in the photograph on the left was part of the RA.65 convoy making for England during a storm off the Norwegian coast. It was taken in March 1945 from the escort carrier *Campania*.

As its share of the booty of war taken from the Italians, the Soviet Northern Fleet received one battleship, nine destroyers and four submarines in 1944 and 1945 from England, together with ten minesweepers, about fifty fast torpedo boats and thirty-six submarine hunters from the USA under the Lend-Lease terms. One of them, *BO 220* (ex USS *SC 1490*) is shown in the photograph above during a major landing operation near Kirkenes in October 1944.

(top) Soviet *BO 220* during landing operation.

(above) 'Liberty ship' of Murmansk convoy RA 65.

(facing page) Tirpitz in Kaa fjord, July 1944.

In January 1942 the *Tirpitz* had been transferred from Wilhelmshaven to Trondheim, where she represented a threat to the Murmansk convoys. This forced the British Admiralty to supplement each pair of convoys with a long-range convoy group consisting of at least two battleships. In an effort to eliminate the threat from the *Tirpitz*, Halifax and Lancaster bombers from RAF Bomber Command attacked the ship in the Fötten-Fjord on 30 March, 27 and 28 April with thirty-three, forty-three and thirty-four aircraft respectively. Seven aircraft were lost, but the ship survived intact. An attack on the *Tirpitz* by the Soviet submarine *K 21*, carried out during the interrupted PQ.17 operation, passed unnoticed by the battleship.

In March 1943 the heavy German ships were moved to the Alta-Fjord, and this change was instrumental in the interruption of the Murmansk convoys in Summer 1943. The raid against Spitzbergen underlined the danger which the *Tirpitz* represented, and in a further effort to eliminate the threat to the winter convoys, the English towed six minisubmarines to Northern Norway. On 22 September 1943 *X 6* and *X 7* succeeded in laying their mines under the *Tirpitz*, and the subsequent explosions forced the ship out of action for six months.

After a Soviet air attack on the *Tirpitz* on 14 February 1944, in which only four of twelve bombers reached their target and achieved a single near-miss, the British tried again. On 3 April the carriers *Victorious* and *Furious* together with four escort carriers carried out a raid involving forty-one Barracuda aircraft. They hit the battleship with fourteen bombs and caused severe damage which cost 108 dead and 184 wounded.

Another seven attempted attacks of a similar type between May and August 1944 failed.

The previous page shows an aerial photograph of the battleship *Tirpitz*, lying in the Norwegian Kaa-Fjord in July 1944.

Twenty-eight RAF Lancaster bombers were transferred to Russia, and on 15 September 1944 they attacked the *Tirpitz* with 6-ton Tallboy bombs. As a result the ship moved to the Lyngen-Fjord near Tromsø. Another attack on 29 October failed, but on 12 November twenty-one Lancasters which had taken off in Scotland struck the *Tirpitz* with several Tallboy bombs, and the battleship capsized. 902 crew members died and 880 were rescued. The picture below shows the wreck in the Lyngen Fjord after the war.

Wreck of *Tirpitz* in Lyngen fjord, photographed post-war.

USS *Arizona* in flames, Pearl Harbor.

War in the Pacific I

7 December 1941–31 July 1942

The Japanese surprise attack on Pearl Harbor on 7 December 1941 signalled the start of the war in the Pacific. The photograph here gives an idea of the devastation, and shows the burning US battleship *Arizona*. America and Japan had viewed each other as potential enemies for many years, and certainly since the Washington Treaty of 1922. The US war plans known as Orange and the Japanese idea of a 'sea ambush' were based on the assumption that the Americans would attempt a naval thrust through the islands of the formerly German colonial region in the central Pacific, presently under Japanese administration by mandate, with the intention of restoring communications with the Philippines. The escalation of tension after Japan established the satellite state of Manchukuo in 1931, and after Japan's expansion onto the Chinese continent in 1937, was too serious to be solved by negotiations alone. In consequence, the Japanese began to embrace the idea of setting up a 'great East-Asian sphere of prosperity', to include the European colonies in Southeast Asia with their wealth of raw materials.

USS *California* sunk at Pearl Harbor.

Admiral Yamamoto, the Japanese Fleet commander, considered the US Pacific Fleet to be the most serious threat to a major Japanese offensive aimed at conquering those regions of Southeast Asia which were rich in raw materials. President Roosevelt had moved the fleet to the naval port of Pearl Harbor in Hawaii in 1940. In the summer of 1941 Yamamoto prevailed against the resistance of the Admiralty staff, and organised a surprise carrier-based air attack on Pearl Harbor as part of his plan of campaign. He formed a battle group consisting of the six most modern aircraft carriers with their 432 aircraft, two battlecruisers, two heavy cruisers and the latest destroyer squadron, and

prepared the remainder of the fleet for support operations during the landings in the South.

American radio intelligence had not cracked the machine cipher named 'purple' which was used for Japanese diplomatic radio traffic, but had penetrated the super-enciphered code known as JN-25 used by the Japanese fleet, although the solution to a new code book introduced on 1 November 1941 was still far from complete. All the news and information which had reached the American Command by early December predicted an imminent Japanese attack in southern Asia. Since the carrier battle group did not feature in the radio messages, and since it had not

been detected as a formation and was not recognised in the North Pacific in any case, the Americans gazed spellbound at southern Asia, ignoring all the indirect signs of an attack against Pearl Harbor. As a result the attack on 7 December 1941 found the Pacific Fleet completely unprepared. In two waves the Japanese aircraft destroyed the American aircraft parked on the airfields and struck at the eight battleships lying in the harbour with their bombs and torpedoes. Within thirty minutes the *Arizona* was a smoking wreck. The *California*, pictured above, was struck by torpedoes and went to the bottom. Three other battleships were sunk, while the three remaining battleships and numerous smaller ships were severely damaged; 2,403 men died and 1,178 were wounded.

Although the eight battleships of the US Pacific Fleet in Pearl Harbor had been eliminated, the two aircraft carriers presently at sea remained intact, together with most of the cruisers and – above all – the logistical installations at Pearl Harbor.

As the indications of an imminent Japanese attack in southern Asia multiplied, Churchill was eager to provide support and cover for the weak American – British – Dutch – Austrian (ABDA) forces in the region under threat, but he was only able to send the battleship *Prince of Wales* and the

old battlecruiser *Repulse* to Singapore because heavy British losses in the Mediterranean (see page 65). When reports were received of Japanese landings on the east coast of Malaya, these two ships put to sea with four old destroyers to attack the Japanese. Japanese submarines made contact with the formation and reported back. Reconnaissance aircraft of the Japanese 22nd Naval Air Squadron took off from Indo-China and located the ships on 11 December 1941. They in turn dispatched twenty-seven twin-engined bombers and sixty-one torpedo aircraft to the position, and both ships were sunk in outstandingly well co-ordinated attacks. The picture below shows a destroyer

alongside the listing *Prince of Wales* rescuing survivors before the ship sank. The destroyers rescued 2,081 men.

Three days earlier, on the morning of 8 December, 192 Japanese bombers and fighter aircraft of the 11th Naval Air Fleet based in Formosa had attacked the Philippine air bases of Clark and Iba and had destroyed twelve American B-17 bombers (Flying Fortresses) on the ground, together with thirty fighter aircraft. At the same time aircraft of the army's 5th Air Division attacked the American airfields on the north coast of the Philippine island of Luzon. This left just the American and Dutch submarines to fight back against the Japanese.

Destroyer rescuing survivors from HMS *Prince of Wales*.

The Japanese troop landings in southern Asia were completed with clockwork precision. The operation began on 8 December 1941 when elements of three divisions were landed on the east coast of Malaya. The photograph above shows Japanese naval infantrymen approaching the beach by boat under fire, after travelling in special landing ships. On 10 December advance divisions landed on small islands and on the north coast of Luzon, the main island of the Philippines, in order to establish airfields for the army air force. They were followed by troops based at Palau, who were landed near Legaspi to block the San Bernardino strait and near Davao on Mindanao in the south of the Philippines. On 22 December the bulk of the 14th Army landed in Lingayen Bay; their

task: to conquer Luzon. On 31 December the major part of the 25th Army travelled to Malaya, some overland through Thailand, some by sea, where it advanced through the jungle towards Singapore. In the meantime small groups had been set down on the north coast of Borneo and on the island of Jolo to the southwest of Mindanao, with the purpose of setting up airfields for the second phase of the Japanese invasion. Cover groups including battlecruisers, heavy cruisers and destroyers stood by.

In January 1942 the second phase of the Japanese landings began, directed primarily against the Dutch East Indies. Paratroopers were dropped on the northern tip of Celebes and near the petroleum centre of Palembang on Sumatra. The Japanese also occupied the

oil ports of Tarakan and Balikpapan on the east coast of Borneo. On 15 February Singapore surrendered. The next target was Java.

On 25 February 1942 the Japanese West group left the Bangka strait with fifty-six transports while the East group left the Macassar strait with forty-one transports, while the carrier fleet took up position to the south of Java. A mixed Allied battle formation consisting of five cruisers and nine destroyers was intercepted by the Japanese cover groups. On 27 and 28 February the Japanese destroyed the Allied fleet formation in the battle of Java Sea, although around 1,200 survivors were rescued. The Japanese landing on Java (pictured above) led to the surrender of the Dutch defenders on 9 March.

(left) Japanese landing on east coast of Malaya.

(above) Japanese landing on Java, Spring 1942.

(right) HMS *Hermes* sinking, April 1942.

In early April the Japanese carrier fleet carried out an attack on Ceylon in which the British carrier *Hermes* (seen burning in the photograph on the right before it sank), two cruisers and numerous merchant ships were sunk. On 6 May 1942 the American defenders of the island fortress of Corregidor in the Manila bay were also obliged to capitulate. The Japanese now controlled the Philippines, Indonesia, Singapore and Hong Kong.

In the meantime the US Pacific Fleet had formed battle groups from their surviving carriers, cruisers and destroyers after the loss of their battleships, but in December 1941 these forces were unable to prevent the fall of the island of Wake. However, from February 1942 the Americans were able to hit the Japanese with attacks against their positions in the Pacific.

Once a successful conclusion of the operations to conquer southern Asia was clearly imminent, fierce arguments broke out in

Japan on the best strategy for the future. The Admiralty staff wanted to continue the offensive by breaking the lines of communication between the USA and Australia. Another group within the Combined Fleet was in favour of hunting down the British Eastern Fleet in the Indian Ocean and thereby gaining naval superiority as the basis for an attack on India or at least Ceylon. However, Yamamoto had concluded that the US aircraft carriers represented the greatest threat, and he planned to entice them into

Battle of the Coral Sea, carrier *Shokaku* hit.

a decisive battle by carrying out an attack on the American Pacific island of Midway. As so often happens, the discussion concluded with the acceptance of all the plans: a thrust into the Indian Ocean in April, the capture of Port Moresby on New Guinea in May, Midway in June, and Fiji, Samoa and New Caledonia in July.

However, on 18 April 1942, while the Japanese carrier fleet was engaged on the

Battle of the Coral Sea: USS *Lexington* explodes.

return voyage from the Indian Ocean, the American carrier *Hornet* carried out a raid on Tokyo and other cities using twin-engined B 25 bombers, from the previously unimaginable range of 600 nautical miles.

On 4 May a Japanese invasion group left Rabaul heading for Port Moresby. Radio intelligence had given the Americans indications that the Japanese were planning operations in the Coral Sea. In response they sent the aircraft carriers *Yorktown* and *Lexington* to the area. On 7 May they locat-

ed the cover group of the Japanese landing fleet and sank the small carrier *Shoho*. The Japanese main fleet included the carriers *Zuikaku* and *Shokaku*, and their aircraft destroyed the US supply vessel *Neosho* and the destroyer *Sims*. On 8 May the Japanese and American carrier groups attacked each other with their aircraft: the Japanese *Shokaku* was hit by three bombs (pictured left), while the *Lexington* was badly damaged and had to be abandoned, exploding after the crew had been rescued (pictured

above). The *Yorktown* was damaged. The battle of the Coral Sea, which was the first occasion when naval fleets fought each other using their carrier aircraft only, without the ships ever gaining sight of each other, was a strategic success for the Americans in spite of their severe losses: the Japanese were forced to give up their attempt at landing in the South of New Guinea, and their penetration into the southwest Pacific was halted.

American Devastator torpedo-planes aboard USS *Enterprise*.

The damage to the *Shokaku* and the loss of many of the *Zuikaku*'s aircraft in the naval battle of Coral Sea did not stop Yamamoto from carrying out his planned attack on Midway even though his carrier fleet was weakened by one third. His highly complex plan included a diversionary raid against Dutch Harbor on the Aleutians carried out by two light carriers, followed by an attack on Midway by the four remaining carriers of the carrier fleet, with the purpose of tempting the US carriers out of Pearl Harbor and drawing them across a line of submarines. In the meantime the landing fleet was intended to land on Midway, while the Aleutian group, the carrier fleet and the battle fleet were to gather for the decisive battle against whatever was left of the American battle formations.

However, an American intelligence officer at Pearl Harbor 'pulled a trick' which led to the Japanese radio operators giving away the target of their attack. The two American carriers were returning from the Tokyo raid, and this trick made it possible for the chief of the Pacific fleet, Admiral Nimitz, to bring them and the *Yorktown*, which had been

repaired in record time after its damage in the Coral Sea battle, into a position flanking the Japanese carrier fleet in good time, ie before the Japanese submarines had arrived. As a result the diversionary raid against the Aleutians did not achieve its intended effect. American spotter aircraft picked up the landing fleet very early – on 3 June 1942. They also detected the carrier fleet early on the fourth, just after the carriers had launched their aircraft, with the result that the aircraft stationed on Midway were already in the air when the Japanese attack struck the island on 4 June. A catapult breakdown on a Japanese cruiser caused such a delay in locating one of the American carrier groups that the Japanese could only re-equip their second wave (which had been armed for a second attack on Midway) for a strike against the American carriers, after the successful defence against the aircraft from Midway and the return of the first wave. However, the attack by the US carrier aircraft also nearly failed. Because the range was so great the torpedo aircraft squadrons were obliged to leave the three carriers without any fighter protection and almost all of them were

shot down by the Japanese Zero fighters, before achieving a single hit.

Although the *Hornet*'s dive-bombers missed their target, those of the *Enterprise* and *Yorktown* arrived virtually at the moment when the Japanese carriers were beginning to launch their fully-laden and fully fuelled squadrons, while the returned first wave was being re-supplied in the hangar decks. Since the carriers were concentrating single-mindedly on the attacking American torpedo aircraft, the dive bombers were able to dive onto the surprised Japanese carriers almost without resistance and within five minutes they had turned the *Akagi*, *Kaga* and *Soryu* into fire-spewing volcanoes. The latter two sank on the same day – 4 June – while the *Akagi* followed them the next morning.

Only the *Hiryu* had managed to escape the attack into a fog bank and now launched its aircraft. The first wave, consisting of eighteen dive-bombers and six fighters, located the *Yorktown*, whose fighters shot down fifteen enemy planes. Even so, the remaining nine aircraft hit the ship with three bombs.

The experienced damage control teams sealed the holes in the flight deck so quickly that when the second wave arrived from the *Hiryu* they believed that they were attacking a different American carrier. This time the *Yorktown* was hit by two torpedoes, causing so much damage that the ship had to be abandoned by her crew.

The photograph on the opposite page shows the *Enterprise*'s Devastator torpedo aircraft squadron before the launch for the operation on 4 June, from which only four machines returned. On the right we see the *Yorktown* listing badly after being abandoned by her crew, and the photograph below shows the *Hiryu* on the afternoon of 4 June after being struck by bombs after carrying out attacks on the *Yorktown*. The *Hiryu* sank on the following day.

(right) Abandoned USS *Yorktown* listing.

(bottom) Japanese carrier *Hiryu* hit by bombs from *Yorktown*'s aircraft.

The chief of the Japanese carrier fleet, Admiral Nagumo, had transferred from the *Akagi* to a cruiser, and he hoped to approach the US carriers during the following night with his battleships and cruisers. However, that same afternoon the two intact American carriers attacked and bombed the *Hiryu* just as she was preparing to launch her third wave of aircraft, and Nagumo decided to retreat. During the night the American Admiral Spruance, who had taken over tactical command, steamed off to the east with his carriers in order to avoid involvement in an artillery battle.

Admiral Yamamoto, far from the battle site on his flagship *Yamato*, decided to break off the Midway operation when he learned of the magnitude of the catastrophe to his carriers. An attempt to bombard the island of Midway using four heavy cruisers during the night of 5 June ended in a collision between the *Mogami* and *Mikuma* when they were trying to evade a US submarine, and on 6 June American carrier aircraft carried out air attacks on the damaged ships. The *Mikuma* was totally destroyed (pictured below) and sank, but the severely damaged *Mogami* was brought home in an admirable exhibition of expert seamanship. In contrast, the *Yorktown*, which had been occupied again by her crew, was sunk on the morning of 7 June by the Japanese submarine *I 168* together with the destroyer *Hammann* which was lying alongside.

The Japanese carried out their landings on the Aleutian islands of Attu and Kiska, which they had intended to form the conclusion of their operation. In addition to the four carriers and the cruiser already mentioned, the cost to the Japanese of the naval air battle of Midway was 253 aircraft and 3,500 men, amongst them many experienced pilots, while the Americans lost one carrier, one destroyer, 150 aircraft and 307 men.

Midway was the turning point of the war in the Pacific. The Japanese never again succeeded in making up for the loss of their most experienced pilots, and failed to re-build a carrier fleet.

Japanese cruiser *Mikuma* sinking after air attack.

Battle of the Atlantic III
11 December 1941–24 May 1943

Since the surface ships which were originally included in the German Z-plan had been cancelled, in September and October 1939 the dockyards received contracts from the German Navy for new 164 U-boats in the form of mobilisation contracts. Dates for start of construction varied according to the situation in the various yards, since some of the stocks could be freed up more quickly than others. By the end of 1939 a total of thirty-eight boats had been laid down, but in the first six months of 1940 the figure rose by a further ninety, by the end of 1940 another ninety-four and in 1941 the total started was 253 boats.

The time taken to complete the submarines also varied. The large yards usually required ten to fourteen months for a boat, while the relatively inexperienced ones sometimes took up to twenty months. In 1939 eighteen boats were completed; in the following year fifty boats, most of them fulfilling prewar contracts. In 1941 the number rose to 198, and in 1942 it rose to 238, which gave a final monthly average of around twenty boats. The most regular suppliers were the Hamburg yard of Blohm & Voss: from the end of 1940 until July 1943 one Type VIIc boat was commissioned at their yard every Thursday. The situation was more difficult for the Germania yard at Kiel which built special types such as the VIID and XB minelayers in addition to the Type VIIc.

Once a submarine was completed there followed a phase lasting several months in which the crew would be trained and the boat worked-up. At the same time residual work was carried out in the yard before the vessel was ready for action. The crew was given a thorough training in keeping contact with surface ships and convoy fighting in the Baltic, before they put to sea at Kiel and sailed via Norway into the Atlantic for their first operation. In 1939 seven boats reached the Atlantic, in 1940 it was 31, in 1941 as many as 98 and in 1942 finally 204. Losses in the corresponding years were nine, twenty-three, thirty-five and eighty-seven.

The picture above shows the Krupp Germania dockyard in Kiel around the turn of the year 1941/42 with the roofed-over stocks in the background. In the fitting-out basin in the foreground left are the large U-boat minelayers *U 118* and *U 119* and behind them three Type VIIc boats. In the background to the right a destroyer can be seen fitting-out.

At first only five U-boats could be spared for Operation Paukenschlag because so many German U-boats were concentrated in the Mediterranean in an attempt to ease the critical situation there (see page 65). Paukenschlag was the operation aimed at destroying merchant shipping off the east coast of America after that country had entered the war in December 1941. By July 1942 numerous other boats had followed, some of them advancing as far as the Gulf of Mexico and the Caribbean. The shipping in those regions was running virtually on a peacetime basis, and the U-boats were enormously successful, not least since the American Chief of Naval Operations, Admiral King, failed to introduce the convoy system in spite of the allies' experience in convoy organisation since September 1941. By the end of July the U-boats had sunk 497 ships amounting to 2,534,305grt in the western Atlantic alone, for the loss of just seven U-boats.

Burning tankers, sinking ships and survivors rescued after long periods in open boats or on the wreckage of their sunken ships – these were the typical images of the time. Corpses were found at sea or were washed up on coasts, yet hardly any photographs of these events have survived. The picture on the left shows the Mexican tanker *Potrero del Llano* enveloped in thick clouds of smoke after being torpedoed off Florida by *U 564* on 14

May 1942, which action led Mexico to declare war. The photograph at the bottom left shows a sinking freighter with floating debris and shipwrecked men swimming in amongst the wreckage.

In the photograph below we see survivors of the American freighter *Ruth Lykes*, which was sunk in the Caribbean by *U 103* on 17 May 1942. The men are receiving information on their position and course from U-boat personnel before they are abandoned to their fate.

The British Admiralty made urgent representations to the US Atlantic Fleet, and as a result convoys began to be introduced in May 1942, initially along the American east

coast, and then by August in the Gulf of Mexico and the Caribbean too.

This change led to a marked reduction in the number of ships travelling singly, with the result that Dönitz withdrew his U-boats from the operational region off the US east coast in May, because the long approach voyages were now considered uneconomic. In the Caribbean the convoy guards were weak and inexperienced at first, and by the end of the year a further 146 ships had been sunk with a total tonnage of 730,209grt. The 'black out' in Bletchley Park (see pages 52/54) did not have a major effect here, as the U-boats were not employed in groups controlled by radio signals.

(top left) Mexican tanker torpedoed by *U 564*.

(below left) Sinking freighter, western Atlantic.

(below) Survivors from US freighter *Ruth Lykes* being given directions by crew of *U 103*.

In 1941/1942 Bedford Bay, outside the Canadian port of Halifax, saw regular gatherings of freighters and tankers of every possible size, as depicted in this aerial photograph, prior to steaming to Great Britain with the weekly fast HX or slow SC convoys. Most convoys comprised thirty to seventy ships, and they they were arranged in six to twelve columns of four to five ships each.

The most valuable ships and the convoy commodore were located in the centre of the formation, and in 1942 the 'escort group' usually consisted of two destroyers and four corvettes. While the German U-boats were operating in the western Atlantic, the convoys had used the shortest Great Circle route, but when Admiral Dönitz withdrew his U-boats from the US east coast and in July 1942 shifted the emphasis to attacking the North Atlantic convoys, the British Submarine Tracking Room found it much more difficult to direct the convoys, as the Ultra teleprinter from Bletchley Park was absent, and the only information on which directions could be worked out was estimates of U-boat formations based on reports of U-boat sightings and radio locations from land-based stations.

Dönitz was often able to exploit decrypted radio messages using the Allied Convoy Code (Naval Cipher 3) supplied by the xB-Dienst. Ten to fifteen or more U-boats would

procedure added to the risk that the U-boats could be located from land, but in spite of this hazard it was considered an indispensable means of directing mobile operations. However, the Germans were unaware that the Allies had by this time developed an apparatus which could exploit the German procedure: High Frequency Direction Finding (HF/DF), which was an automatic shipborne short-wave radio locating device. It used a trapezoid Adcock antenna fitted to the mast tip and could locate a U-boat transmitting a brief signal within a range of 30 nautical miles. The Escort Commander, who acted as tactical leader of the convoy, was then able to order a destroyer to steam along the bearing until its radar device detected the U-boat keeping contact. The U-boat would be forced to dive, but the destroyer's Asdic echo locating device would pick up its position and keep it under water by dropping depth charges until the convoy had altered course.

This method was successfully used for the first time on 16 June 1942, when a German U-boat lost contact with the convoy ONS.102. The Canadian destroyer *Restigouche* (pictured below with its Adcock

HF/DF antenna on the after mast and the 1.5m Type 286 radar on the forward masthead) detected *U 94* and forced it away. From then on the Allies avoided many a convoy battle by this method.

A further important innovation was the introduction of the Hedgehog, a box from which twenty-four small depth charges could be fired forward. These small charges only detonated if they struck a U-boat, and in consequence they did not disrupt the Asdic location system by turbulence, as was the case when a depth charge missed its target and then exploded.

At this time the Allies' greatest handicap was the 'air hole', that area in the middle of the North Atlantic which was out of range of any aircraft stationed in Northern Ireland, Iceland and Newfoundland. Eventually, the problem was solved with the introduction of Very Long Range (VLR) Liberators which were prepared specifically to meet this challenge, but not until the critical period of March 1943 when forty-five of the long-range aircraft became available.

(left) Convoys assembling at Halifax 1941/2.

(below) Canadian destroyer *Restigouche*.

steam in the formation of a reconnaissance line on the search for convoys, first to the west, where they would be re-fuelled by one of the new U-boat tankers known as Milchkuh, then turn and cruise back towards the east.

If a U-boat sighted a convoy it would broadcast a contact signal, and the German U-boat Command at Kernevel near Lorient then used this signal as the basis for an order to the other boats to attack the convoy. This

In December 1942 Bletchley Park succeeded in breaking the U-boat cipher Triton when it received the weather short signal book obtained from *U 559* in the Mediterranean. However, there were now so many U-boat formations in the North Atlantic that the procedure of diverting convoys was no longer an effective method of defence. This was emphasised by the fate of the four convoys which crossed the Atlantic in March 1943, of which 20 per cent of the merchant ships were sunk. From now on the newly formed Support Groups and the VLR aircraft were employed to push through those convoys perceived to be in danger from German U-boat formations as a result of Ultra decrypts. The Allied policy was to force them underwater and then sink them when they were forced to surface.

An example of this was the sinking of *U 175* on 17 April 1943 close to the convoy HX.233. The photograph on the left shows the US Coast Guard cutter *Spencer* acting as lead ship of Escort Group A.3, receiving a line fired across by a propellant cartridge. One of Spencer's boats is seen below close to *U 175*, which has been forced to surface after being damaged by depth charges. The U-boat eventually sank, and in the photograph on the right survivors from the U-boat dangle on ropes let down from the *Spencer*'s deck.

(above) US Coast Guard cutter *Spencer*. *(below)* Boat from *Spencer* alongside crippled *U 175*.

(right) Survivors from *U 175* picked up by *Spencer*.

War in the Pacific II
1 August 1942–30 September 1943

The Allied Europe First strategy tied up a large part of the US fleet for Operation Torch – the landing in North Africa (see page 120) – and allowed only limited forces to remain in the Pacific. Yet Admiral King was emphatic that an offensive should be carried out in the South Pacific in order to deny the Japanese any chance to recover.

After their defeat at Midway the Japanese had been forced to abandon their plans for the conquest of Fiji, New Caledonia and Samoa, but they were in the process of securing their main base of Rabaul on the formerly German island of New Britain by carrying out landings on the coast of New Guinea, and by expanding their airfield on the southernmost Solomon island of Guadalcanal. For a period of six months the struggle for this airfield determined the course of the war in the Pacific.

On 7 August 1942 the Americans opened up their offensive by landing the reinforced 1st Marine Division on Tulagi and on the opposite north coast of Guadalcanal, driving the Japanese from the airfield which they now named Henderson Field after a fallen American pilot. The possession of Henderson Field was the focal point for a battle which lasted half a year.

The Japanese immediately responded with air attacks by land-based aircraft from Rabaul, which persuaded the Americans to withdraw their transport fleet. Two American-Australian task forces, each comprising three heavy cruisers and six destroyers, were left to cover the access routes to the landing area on both sides of Savo island.

During the night of 9 August a Japanese battle group consisting of five heavy cruisers, two small cruisers and one destroyer outmanoeuvred the US destroyer *Blue*, which was guarding the southern entrance between Savo and Guadalcanal, and surprised first the southern Allied cruiser group, whose flagship had left for a conference of Allied commanders, and then the northern group too. In a dramatic night-time battle near Savo Island the Japanese demonstrated the superiority of their optical fire control, while the American radar devices failed, and without suffering major damage the Japanese sank the US cruisers *Vincennes* and *Quincy* and set the *Astoria* and the Australian *Canberra* alight; both ships had to be sunk the following morning. The photograph below shows the burning *Canberra* with the US destroyers *Patterson* and *Blue*, which rescued 680 survivors from her. In total the Allies lost 1,023 dead and 709 wounded at Savo island.

Cruiser HMAS *Canberra* burning, Savo Island.

The Americans pulled their ships out of the landing area, with the result that the 16,000 marines who had been landed on Guadalcanal were left to their own devices for a while.

The Japanese began to bring up smaller reinforcements and sought to tie down the Americans by carrying out air attacks from Rabaul. On 24 August a reinforcement transport from Rabaul arrived at Guadalcanal carrying 1,500 men, covered by the Japanese fleet consisting of two large carriers, three battleships, eight heavy cruisers and two light cruisers as well as twenty-two destroyers, which had been cruising to the east of the Solomons. The Americans had three task forces to support their marines on Guadalcanal, each one consisting of an aircraft carrier guarded by a battleship, five heavy cruisers, two light cruisers and eighteen destroyers.

The aircraft from the US carriers *Saratoga* and *Enterprise* failed to find the Japanese convoy and on 24 August in an air battle close to the eastern Solomons only managed to sink the light carrier *Ryujo* – a member of a diversionary formation – while the aircraft of the Japanese carriers *Shokaku* and *Zuikaku* inflicted serious damage on the *Enterprise*.

The Japanese submarine squadrons which had been sent to combat the US carrier task forces now achieved their only major success in a fleet action – the purpose for which they had actually been built. On 26 September 1942 *I 26* torpedoed the *Saratoga*, and on 15 September *I 19* used a Long Lance six-torpedo fan to hit the carrier *Wasp* with three torpedoes, the distant battleship *North Carolina* with one torpedo, and the destroyer *O'Brien* with one torpedo. The *Wasp* was set alight and had to be abandoned, as shown in the top photograph, while the other damaged ships were towed away. This incident meant that there were no carriers left available to cover American operations. The only aircraft available to carry out attacks were the land-based aircraft of the Americans at Guadalcanal and of the Japanese at Rabaul, which attempted to attack the reinforcement convoys of their opponents. The photograph on the right shows a Japanese torpedo aircraft, its torpedo visible under the fuselage, passing the US cruiser *Northampton* on its approach to attack a larger ship.

(top) USS *Wasp* abandoned.

(bottom) Japanese plane over USS *Northampton*.

On 12 October 1942 an American task force forced a Japanese bombardment force to turn back in a night battle near Cape Esperance. The Japanese fleet had now been strengthened by carriers which had been repaired in Japan and brought back to the region, and Admiral Yamamoto planned a new attack aimed at re-taking Henderson Field and driving the Americans from Guadalcanal, but at this he was unsuccessful. However, in the battle of Santa Cruz on 25 and 26 October the Japanese achieved a tactical success when they again managed to damage the repaired *Enterprise*. Massive AA fire from the new battleship *South Dakota* (visible in the background in the picture on the left) and from other ships prevented the *Enterprise* (foreground) suffering mortal damage, but the severely hit new carrier *Hornet* was lost. Once again the Americans did not have a single serviceable aircraft carrier.

Other types of weapons also made their mark. On 25 October the large troop transport *President Coolidge*, with sections of two US divisions on board, struck a mine and sank, but since this occurred inshore, all the 4,000 soldiers on board were able to save themselves (pictured below) with the exception of two.

(left) Battle of Santa Cruz.

(below) Troops abandoning *President Coolidge*.

In November 1942 the battle for Guadalcanal resulted in severe losses to ships and men of both sides. Again and again battle formations consisting of cruisers and destroyers and even battleships engaged each other in their attempts to fire at enemy positions or Henderson Field, and to land reinforcements and supplies on the island. Time and again bitter night battles raged at very close range.

In the great night battles off Guadalcanal which took place on the 12, 13, and 14/15 November, in the air attacks, and in a successful torpedo attack by eight Japanese destroyers against a cruiser group in the night battle of Tassafaronga, the Japanese lost two battlecruisers, one cruiser, three destroyers and ten transports, while the Americans lost four cruisers and eight destroyers, and three more cruisers were torpedoed. In fact, the Japanese never succeeded in reinforcing their troops sufficiently, and by 9 February 1943 they had evacuated Guadalcanal, taking 11,706 men with them.

After the expansion of their air bases the Americans initiated their advance on Rabaul in March 1943 by landing troops on islands of the central Solomons and the north coast of the Papuan peninsula, in each case seeking to circumvent powerful Japanese positions. In

US destroyer firing on Japanese forces off Vella Lavella.

July, August and October these actions resulted in continual night-time battles in which both sides suffered losses. The photograph above was taken on 21 October and shows an American destroyer firing on Japanese forces in the vicinity of the Solomons island of Vella Lavella.

In the North Pacific the Japanese had occupied the Aleutian islands of Attu and Kiska after the conclusion of the battle of Midway. Gradually they reinforced their numbers on these islands until by Spring 1943 they had 2,500 and 5,400 men stationed there respectively.

The Americans shifted their bases from Dutch Harbor to Adak and Amchitka initially, close to Kiska, and tried to intercept the Japanese supply system. During their operations, on 26 March 1943, the only daylight artillery battle between cruisers took place at the Komandorski islands, in which the USS *Salt Lake City* was severely damaged.

After repeated attacks by land-based bombers and heavy bombardment from two battleships, American army divisions landed on Attu on 11 May 1943, and by 29 May they had overcome the Japanese defenders, who literally continued to fight to the last man, suffering 2,351 casualties in all. Only twenty-eight Japanese allowed themselves to be taken prisoner. The Americans suffered 600 dead and 1,200 wounded. Many breakdowns and accidents in the loading of the transports and in tactical operations on land provided the Americans with valuable experience for their future amphibious actions.

American aircraft, submarines and ships, which were now able to use Attu as a base, located between the Japanese bases on the Kurile islands and Kiska, were increasingly successful in halting the flow of support to Kiska, and eventually the Japanese decided to evacuate the island. This they did in late July, completely unnoticed by the Americans. They exploited foggy weather and completed a master-stroke of tactical planning in their departure. When the Americans began their landing on the island on 15 August 1943 (pictured below), with almost one hundred ships and 34,426 American and Canadian troops, they found the island abandoned.

US and Canadian troops landing on the abandoned Kiska island.

Immediately after Pearl Harbor the American submarines had initiated an unrestricted submarine war against Japanese shipping, but frequent torpedo failures frustrated them, and they achieved almost no success against the Japanese operation in the south; during 1942 and 1943 they only inflicted occasional damage on warships. They were based in Hawaii and operated off Japan and in the former German colonial region, although some were based in Australia and the southwest Pacific, where they attempted to disrupt the Japanese supply traffic to the Solomons and New Guinea.

As their numbers slowly rose, and their weapons steadily improved, they also learned to make better use of intelligence from radio intelligence systems, and their success rate gradually improved. By July 1942 they had sunk only sixty-four ships, but by the end of 1942 the American submarines had destroyed a further seventy-five, and in 1943 they accounted for a further 204. The photograph below is of a view through the periscope of an American submarine, in whose sights is a Japanese freighter sunk by the submarine in April 1943. The bottom picture shows an American submarine fitted out with guns after a refit to the conning tower.

(below) Sinking Japanese freighter seen through US submarine periscope.
(bottom) US submarine with enhanced gun armament.

War in the Indian Ocean

Rendezvous between German *U 180* and Japanese *I 29*, south of Madagascar.

1942–1945

By the end of 1941 the Indian Ocean had only seen a few sorties by Italian destroyers and submarines from Massaua in Abyssinia into the Red Sea, and some operations by German surface raiders. In April 1942 the Japanese carried out raids on Ceylon (see page 97) and in the Gulf of Bengal, in which twenty-three merchant ships were destroyed in addition to a number of warships. In all Japanese submarines had sunk a total of forty-four ships by this time.

In conjunction with the the Japanese army's penetration into Burma and the German-Italian offensive in North Africa this Japanese raid made the Allied Command staffs fearful that they were in danger of losing maritime superiority in the Indian Ocean, and that the supply routes to the Middle East and the Soviet Union via Iran would be cut.

The Vichy-French island of Madagascar posed a certain threat to the Allies, and on 5 May 1942 the British landed troops on the northern coast of the island near Diego Suarez, which soon broke down the initial resistance. One of Japan's diversionary actions for the Midway operation (see page 100) was to send a group of four cruiser submarines supported by two auxiliary cruisers to search for the British fleet in the western Indian Ocean. A submarine spotter aircraft sighted the British at Diego Suarez. On 30 May the Japanese dispatched midget submarines to the attack, and they torpedoed the battleship *Ramillies* and a tanker. By 25 July the Japanese ships had sunk twenty-five merchant ships in the area around Madagascar. Japanese cruiser submarines operating singly continued these operations until autumn 1944, sinking a further fifty-four ships.

In October 1942 a formation of German U-boats attacked merchant shipping off South Africa for the first time, and thereby forced the Allies to adopt the convoy system for the Indian Ocean. Other groups of U-boats and individual boats followed, and after autumn 1943 they operated from the Japanese base of Penang in the Malacca straits. German U-boats sank 164 merchant ships in total in the Indian Ocean. From 1942 to 1945 Japanese, German and Italian submarines carried out a series of voyages between Penang and France, the purpose of which was to exchange raw materials and plans for weapons systems. The German U-boat *U 180* was one of the boats involved. In the photograph above she is seen meeting the Japanese cruiser submarine *I 29* on 26 April 1943 south of Madagascar. She is taking on board important raw materials and two Japanese officers for passage to Kiel – for instruction in submarine building – and at the same time is transferring to the Japanese gold bars, design drawings for U-boats and the Indian politician Subhas Chandra Bose, who collaborated with the Axis powers, and who travelled to Japan to organise an Indian army against the British.

Allied air raid on Surabaja, Java.

When the Japanese offensive into India failed to take place, and the Germans began to withdraw in North Africa after the battle of El Alamein (see page 68), the immediate dangers to the Near East and India appeared to be averted, at least temporarily, and from then on the Indian Ocean remained a secondary theatre of war, for which only limited naval forces were made available. The British Eastern Fleet had always consisted of obsolescent ships and had escaped to East Africa in 1942. By the end of 1943 the fleet comprised one old battleship, one escort carrier, eight cruisers, eleven destroyers and a number of smaller units. The naval war in the Indian Ocean was waged primarily by British and Dutch submarines.

In the summer of 1943 Churchill pushed for an intensification of the war in the southeast Asian region on land, on sea and in the air, and in August he carried through the appointment of the young Vice-Admiral Lord Mountbatten as Supreme Allied Commander South East Asia. The Eastern Fleet was moved back to Ceylon. Early in 1944 the fleet was reinforced by three modernised battleships, two aircraft carriers, two cruisers and two flotillas of modern destroyers, which had been withdrawn from other regions, and these were followed by further allied ships of all classes.

On 4 February 1944 the Japanese army launched an offensive 'to liberate India', supported by S Ch Bose's National Army, which had been established by Japan and consisted of Indian prisoners of war. However, after the capture of Imphal in March the operation came to a standstill and failed altogether in April. In an effort to place the Japanese under pressure in Indonesia, the Eastern Fleet, which had been strengthened by the addition of the battleship *Valiant* and the French battleship *Richelieu*, several escort carriers and an American battle formation including the large carrier *Saratoga*, carried out a raid against Sabang on the northern tip of Sumatra on 19 April 1944 using British and American carrier aircraft. On 17 May another attack was made against Surabaja on Java, and the photograph above shows bombs bursting during this attack.

In June the Eastern Fleet carried out a number of raids against targets in Sumatra, in an attempt to divert Japanese attention from the imminent attack on the Mariana Islands by the Americans (see page 171). In July there followed further attacks by the carriers *Victorious* and *Indomitable* against Sabang, followed up by bombardments from three battleships. The photograph at top right shows, in the wake of the battleship *Queen Elizabeth*, the flagship of the Commander of the Eastern Fleet, Admiral Somerville, her sister ship *Valiant* in the foreground and the Free-French *Richelieu*, which had undergone a complete refit in the USA, behind.

In August 1944 the new battleship *Howe* and the carrier *Illustrious* entered the Indian Ocean and took part in a raid against Padang on the southwest coast of Sumatra, followed by further attacks at intervals of four weeks.

After advances by the British, American and Chinese formations in Burma, which were well supported thanks to the build-up of a powerful American air fleet, the Japanese slowly began to withdraw from Burma in January 1945. On the Burmese coast Task Force 64 supported the actions of the XV Indian Corps by carrying out a series of troop landings. In the centre picture the Australian destroyer *Norman* fires on Japanese positions on 30 January 1945 during a landing on the Burmese island of Ramree.

When Mandalay was captured on 20 March 1945 the Burma Strait to China was re-opened, and the British advance towards Rangoon from the north quickly gained ground, supported on 1 May by a landing from the south which forced the Japanese to evacuate the town. The bottom photograph was taken on 2 May and shows a British jeep pulling a gun from an LCT onto land through the mud of the Rangoon delta.

In late 1944 the modern ships of the Eastern Fleet were transferred into the Pacific.

(top) Battleships HMS *Queen Elizabeth* and the French *Richelieu*.

(centre) Australian destroyer *Norman*.

(bottom) Landings on the Rangoon delta.

The Mediterranean II
1 November 1942–8 May 1945

The American Chiefs of Staff were eager to push the Europe first strategy to a successful conclusion by carrying out a landing in France as early as possible, preferably in 1942, but in any case not later than 1943. However, the British considered such an operation as impracticable with the forces available, and instead suggested landings in Morocco and Algeria in an attempt to drive the Axis powers out of Africa, in conjunction with an offensive from Egypt, and thereby open up the Mediterranean. This plan was given priority, and on 8 November 1942 Operation Torch began with the landing of 34,305 men of the US 3rd and 9th Divisions on the Moroccan west coast near Casablanca. Pictured below is the American aircraft carrier *Ranger* on the morning before the landing, with fighters and dive bombers on deck and two destroyers in the background. In the Oran area British ships landed 39,000 men of the US 1st Division and half of the 1st Tank Division. Near Algiers further British ships landed 33,000 men consisting of the other half of the US 1st Armoured Division, part of the 34th division and part of the British 78th Division.

At first the French resisted bitterly, firing from the ships lying in the ports and the coastal batteries, and this action cost 803 dead and over 1,000 wounded before Admiral Darlan signed an armistice on 10 November, with the secret agreement of Marshal Petain. The landings in North Africa took the German Command by surprise, but they did respond quickly. As early as 9 November 1942 the German 5th Paratroop Regiment was landed in Tunis by air, and on the following day they occupied the port of Bizerta,

Carrier USS *Ranger* and two destroyers before Operation Torch.

Scuttled French ships in Toulon.

where 12,000 French soldiers were taken prisoner. On 11 November German troops marched into the previously unoccupied part of France, although they steered clear of the military port of Toulon. At the same time the Italians occupied Corsica. Luftwaffe groups were brought in and they began to attack the landing fleets with the support of U-boats.

By mid-November the Allies had lost one escort carrier, one AA ship, three destroyers, six smaller vessels and eighteen transports.

The Allied attack on Tunisia failed, and although French troops went over to the Allied side on 16 November and participated in the fighting, Rommel's Africa Korps was able to withdraw to Tunisia via Libya.

The Germans recognised the fact that the French fleet lying at Toulon would go over to the Allied side, and to prevent this happening the German II SS Armoured Corps moved into the port on 27 November

1942, but they were unable to prevent the French fleet being scuttled. Three battleships, one seaplane carrier, seven cruisers, twenty-five destroyers, five torpedo boats, sixteen submarines and many smaller ships sank and were thereby kept out of the clutch of the Germans. Five submarines escaped. In the photograph we see the capsized cruiser *Marseillaise* in the foreground, and heavy cruisers burning in the background. The vessel on the right is the *Algerie*.

German and Italian ships continued to transport supplies to the troops fighting in Tunisia, but the rate of loss on these voyages increased steadily as the Allies gained aerial and naval superiority. In early May 1943 they were stopped altogether. On 12 May the Africa army, consisting of 250,000 Germans and Italians, was forced to surrender at the Tunisian bridgehead, where they were confined in a very small area.

In December 1942 the British Chief of the Imperial General Staff, General Sir Alan Brooke, convinced Churchill that a landing in France could still not be countenanced for August 1943. His reasons were that there was no end in sight to the fighting in North Africa, and that the naval situation was not favourable. In a summit conference held at Casablanca in January 1943 the American Chiefs of Staff had to give way to these arguments, and it was decided to use the forces located in the Mediterranean for a landing on Sicily in July 1943.

At first, priority was given to combatting the German U-boat menace and continuing the bombing campaign. Preparations were made for Operation Husky, but new controversies arose. Eventually, the Commander of the British 8th Army, General Montgomery,

prevailed, and a concentrated landing in southeastern Sicily was agreed. This operation required the preparation of 2,311 transports and landing vessels and 279 warships for support purposes, and this was a major organisational task. The picture below shows US troops destined for Sicily embarking on LCIs in a north African port.

At dawn on 10 July 1943 three British, one Canadian and three American divisions stormed on land. The picture at the top of the opposite page shows British soldiers landing in the vicinity of Syracuse through a choppy sea, and the town was captured undamaged the following day. 116,000 British and 66,000 American solders were landed on Sicily in total.

Italian and German submarines fought against the action from the sea, but they

were only able to sink six ships and torpedo two cruisers whilst losing eleven of their own vessels. German air attacks proved to be more effective, and fifteen ships succumbed to them. The picture at bottom right shows German bombs exploding close to American ships off the Sicilian coast.

The German and Italian defenders retreated to a bridgehead around Messina, fighting a rearguard action, but they were unable to prevent several further allied landings, each overlapping the previous one. From 3 to 17 August German and Italian ferries and boats evacuated 101,569 soldiers, 47 tanks, 135 guns, 9,382 vehicles and 17,000 tons of munitions, fuel and materials to the Italian mainland via the Messina strait, running at night and with constant support from AA guns.

(above) US ships under air attack off Sicily

(top) British troops landing near Syracuse.

(left) US troops in North Africa embarking for Sicily, July 1943.

While the heavy fighting was taking place on Sicily, Mussolini was being deposed by the Grand Council of Fascism, and on 25 July 1943 Marshal Badoglio took over the reins of government. Although he publicly declared that Italy would continue fighting, in secret he initiated negotiations with the Allies, and on 3 September Italy signed the unconditional surrender, which was to come into force on 8 September.

Hitler responded to the fall of Mussolini by giving the order to evacuate Sicily and by reinforcing the German troops in Italy. He also ordered that preparations be made to neutralise the Italian troops if Italy should withdraw from the war.

On the Allied side new discussions were held on the strategy to be followed. At the summit conferences Trident and Quadrant in May and August 1943 the Chief of Staff of the US Army, General Marshall, demanded once more that forces should be moved from the Mediterranean to prepare for an invasion of France. The Chief of Naval Operations, Admiral King, pushed for a transfer of amphibious formations into the Pacific. The British Chiefs of Staff argued that defeating Italy by landing troops on the mainland would weaken the Germans in France so severely that an invasion of that country would then be possible in the spring of 1944, when the forces should be sufficient for the purpose. The elimination of Italy from the war, which was now foreseeable because of the negotiations which had already been held, finally turned the scales in favour of continuing operations in the Mediterranean by means of a landing near Salerno, to the south of Naples, to coincide with the Italian surrender on 8 September 1943.

On 3 September two British divisions travelled from Messina and landed on the tip of Calabria in an attempt to tie down the German formations in the south, but this plan was not successful. On the afternoon of 8 September the Allied Commander, General Eisenhower, announced the Italian surrender, and in accordance with the negotiated conditions the Italian fleet put to sea from La Spezia and Genoa in order to surrender. The fleet consisted of three battleships, six cruisers and eight destroyers. Eleven German Do 217 bombers carrying FX-1200 remote-controlled bombs attacked the formation in the Bonifacio Strait between Corsica and Sardinia and hit the battleship *Roma*, which suffered a gigantic explosion (bottom left) and sank. The *Italia* was also damaged, but on 10 September 1943 the remaining ships were escorted by the British Mediterranean Fleet and taken to Malta, where three elderly Italian battleships, two cruisers and two destroyers from Taranto and Italian Adriatic ports had already arrived.

(below left) Italian battleship *Roma* hit by German glider-bomb.

(below right) US troops boarding landing craft from *Samuel Chase* off Salerno.

British and American landing ships landing troops near Salerno.

On the morning of 9 September 1943 the Allied 5th Army consisting of three British and two American divisions landed on the beach between Salerno and Paestum, together with 150 tanks, 144 field guns, and 224 light guns and howitzers. The landing fleet consisted of 150 large and 222 small landing ships as well as 99 smaller vessels. The landing was supported by six aircraft carriers, four battleships, one monitor, seven cruisers and forty-seven destroyers. In the picture on the left can be seen troops transferring from the US passenger steamer *Samuel Chase*, which had been converted into an attack transport, to the landing boats which had been disembarked for the run to the beach near Salerno. The photograph above shows one of the first three British tank landing ships of the Boxer class (centre) and two American vessels *LST 16* (left) and *LST 379* (right) landing troops, vehicles and Sherman tanks. The forces which landed near Salerno encountered the determined resistance of the German 16th Armoured Division, which was equipped with one hundred tanks, fifty-

five assault guns, thirty-six howitzers and eight 88mm AA guns.

In the northern sector the British divisions fought their way on land under the protection of the ships' artillery. Initially, the Americans suffered quite severe losses, but eventually they gained their bridgehead in the course of the day. However, although the German defenders were initially inferior in number, the Allies failed to exploit this weakness in order to advance deeper. The German Commander in Italy, Field Marshal Kesselring, hoped to be able to crush the bridgehead with the German divisions approaching from the south, retreating before the British 8th Army, and the German troops now available after the neutralisation of the Italian troops in central Italy. However, the 8th Army had received further reinforcement through the amphibious landing of the British 1st Airborne Division at Taranto on 9 September. The Germans now numbered six tank and mechanised divisions with their added reinforcements, although the divisions were weak. In the period from

12 to 14 September they now carried out continual counter-attacks which put the Allied troops under considerable pressure – especially the American VI Corps. It was only with the ceaseless fire of the Allied ships' guns that the Allies overcame this critical situation. On 16 September the first advance guard of the British 8th Army reached the bridgehead, and on the 18th Kesselring was obliged to order a gradual withdrawal. Even so, it was not until 1 October 1943 that the Allies were able to reach Naples, whose port facilities had been severely damaged by Allied air attacks and explosive charges set by the Germans. On 8 October the allied offensive was held up at the Volturno and came to a complete halt on 15 November outside Monte Cassino after making very slow progress. Allied hopes of capturing Rome before the end of 1943 had been dashed and the Allies' battle for Italy continued to occupy warships and tie up landing ships.

Direct bomb hit on cruiser USS *Savannah* off Salerno.

It was only thanks to the heavy fire support of the British and American ships that the Allied troops landed near Salerno were able to withstand the keen German counter-attacks. At the same time the ships had to submit to numerous German air attacks. When the battleship *Warspite* and the aircraft carrier *Formidable* were approaching the area they were narrowly missed by torpedo aircraft. The monitor *Abercrombie* played an important role with its 15in guns, but on 9 September 1943 the ship struck a mine and was put out of action. During the night of the eleventh the destroyer *Rowan* was sunk in an attack by an S-boat. On the following day the Germans began heavy air attacks using FX-1200 remote-controlled bombs and HS-293 glide bombs: the US cruiser *Savannah* received a direct hit (above), and her sister ship *Philadelphia* suffered damage in a near-miss. On 14 September aircraft inflicted serious damage on the British cruiser *Uganda*, two destroyers and the *Philadelphia* again, and the hospital ship *Newfoundland* was sunk. On the 15th the battleships *Valiant* and *Warspite* joined the action, but both ships were hit by FX-1200 bombs and suffered severe damage. As of 2 October German U-boats were able to use the new Zaunkönig torpedoes, and they sank two destroyers, two minesweepers and seven transports off the Allied beach head and from supply convoys off the Algerian coast.

In the period between 10 to 20 September small German vessels evacuated 26,000 men, 2,300 vehicles and 5,000 tons of materials from Sardinia to Corsica via the Straits of Bonifacio, and after concluding a standstill agreement with the Italian garrison they were transferred to the mainland by the air and sea route by 5 October 1943. In the meantime French submarines and ships carried 7,139 French troops from Algiers to Ajaccio on Corsica over numerous separate journeys. The Germans laid mine barrages in an attempt to secure the coasts and to block incursions by Allied destroyers and PT-boats.

After the Italian surrender had been announced, fighting broke out between the weak German and the stronger Italian units on Rhodes, and in response the British sent small battle groups and commandos to support the Italians on the Dodecanese islands, travelling on light vessels. Once the Italians on Rhodes had surrendered on 11 September 1943 the Germans began to transfer their prisoners to Piraeus by ship. British destroyers had been moved from the central Mediterranean to the Aegean, and they attempted to reinforce the Dodecanese garrisons and prevent movement of the German transports. On 23 September the Italian transport *Donizetti* was sunk off Rhodos, with the loss of 1,576 prisoners.

On 26 September the Germans began operations aimed at regaining the Dodecanese, and the first step was air attacks in which one British, one Greek and one Italian destroyer were sunk at Leros. On 3 October German submarine hunters and small ships carried troops to Kos with air support, and 1,388 British and 3,145 Italians were taken prisoner. On 7 October a British battle formation destroyed a German convoy bound for Kos, rescuing 1,207 survivors. Reinforcements to the German Luftwaffe and mine barrages laid by minelayers presented additional problems to the Allied operations.

By this time the Germans had requisitioned the Italian destroyers and torpedo boats lying at Piraeus and had put four of them into serviceable condition. With their help and powerful air support they succeeded in landing troops on Leros and Samos in the period 10 to 24 November 1943. These troops forced 3,200 British and 5,350 Italians to surrender on Leros, and 2,500 Italians on Samos. The Allied ships employed for the evacuation eventually had to bow to German air superiority and leave the fight against the German supply lines to the submarines.

The photograph here shows the German prize torpedo boat *TA 15* (formerly *Francesco Crispi*) in the port of Piraeus after transporting British and Indian prisoners there from Leros.

It was not until the Soviets advanced into Roumania and Bulgaria in August 1944 that the British won back the initiative and forced the Germans to evacuate Greece.

British and Indian prisoners from Leros in Pireaus; German *TA 15* behind.

Landings at Anzio.

In December 1943 the failure of the Allies' attempts to break through the German Gustav position at the Garigliano and outside Monte Cassino caused Churchill to suggest a large-scale amphibious landing behind the German lines in an effort to interrupt the supply lines and capture Rome quickly. The Allied landing ships in the Mediterranean were due to be transferred to England, but on 28 December Roosevelt agreed that they should remain in the Mediterranean for three further weeks.

On the morning of 22 January 1944 three infantry landing ships, thirty-three tank landing ships and fifty-one smaller landing vessels landed the British 1st division at Anzio, 30 miles south of Rome, and five infantry landing ships, fifty-one tank landing ships and 104 smaller landing vessels landed

the American 3rd Division. They met only weak resistance and soon formed a bridgehead. The photograph here shows infantry landing boats (LCIs) landing troops of the US 3rd Division near Anzio. At front right on the beach is an amphibious vehicle (Amtrack), on the left and right the two British landing craft *LCI 274* and *LCI 356*, and in the centre the American *LCI 39* and *LCI 20*, the latter in flames after being struck by a German bomb. The commanding officer of the US VI Corps, General Lucas, did not push inland deeply enough on the first day, and failed to interrupt the main German supply route from Rome to the front. Kesselring was able quickly to bring up units of the German 14th Army, which counter-attacked and surrounded the bridgehead. The Allies brought up four more divi-

sions, increasing the Allied strength at the bridgehead to 68,886 men, 237 tanks and 508 guns in the first week, but even this could not turn the situation round. The German Luftwaffe immediately began heavy attacks against the landing fleet, and in the first few days one AA ship, one destroyer, two minesweepers and two landing vessels were lost to mines. German fighter-bombers, Do 217 and Ju-88 aircraft with torpedoes, bombs and Hs-293 glider bombs sank the cruiser *Spartan*, a destroyer, two transports and the ambulance ship *St David*, and two destroyers were seriously damaged. Two German U-boats carried out five attacks in the first week, penetrating into the landing region, but they all failed.

Reserves were brought up to reinforce the German 14th Army, and from 16 to 18 February 1944 they attacked the bridgehead near Anzio and tried to force the Allied forces back into the sea. However, after initial successes the attack became bogged down. The Allies were obliged to reinforce their troops at the bridgehead again, which once more meant that supply ships and warships had to be kept in the Mediterranean for artillery support when the intention had been to transfer them to England in preparation for the invasion of France. A further destroyer was sunk by German air attacks, and U-boats sank the cruiser *Penelope*, one transport and four tank landing ships.

From the second half of February until early May 1944 the battle for the positions near Cassino and the Garigliano between the German defenders and the American, French, South African, Canadian, British, Polish, New Zealand and Indian divisions dragged on, and no advance was made at the Anzio bridgehead either. It was only on 13 May that the French achieved the breakthrough, after three days of heavy fighting, and on 25 May the link to the Anzio bridgehead was created. At Anzio the British had lost 9,200 dead, wounded and missing, and the Americans 29,000. Two thousand Germans were taken prisoner in the three days of fighting which led to the break-out

from the bridgehead. The photograph below shows some of the German prisoners waiting behind rapidly erected barbed wire fences for their transport.

The Germans were forced to abandon Rome on 4 June 1944, and in early August they withdrew, fighting a rearguard action, to the Gotenstellung position running from Pisa through Florence to Ancona.

In August 1943, in the preparation for the invasion of the French Channel coast, the American Chiefs of Staff had already planned a provisional landing in the South of France, although the British would have preferred to set up an offensive in the Balkans.

German prisoners taken at Anzio.

(above) US troops landing in the south of France.

The shipping situation necessitated a postponement of the landing in southern France until after the invasion on the Channel coast. Thus it was not until 15 August 1944 that the landing was carried out. After heavy air attacks involving 1,300 aircraft, 396 transport aircraft dropped 5,000 paratroopers between Cannes and Toulon. Landings on the coast followed, in which 86,575 men, 12,250 vehicles and 46,140 tons of materials were landed. In the picture above LCIs are seen landing troops of the US 7th Army, while in the picture on the left the French cruiser *Montcalm*, one of the ships employed for artillery support, approaches the coast. The defending German 19th Army soon withdrew into the Rhone valley, and 57,000 men were taken prisoner.

French cruiser *Montcalm*.

Biscay, the Channel and the North Sea

1 January 1942–31 August 1944

The German battleships *Scharnhorst* and *Gneisenau* had entered Brest after their Atlantic operations. The danger to them and to the heavy cruiser *Prinz Eugen* from Allied air attacks, and the impossibility of training in the Bay of Biscay, caused a change of plan; early in 1942 it was decided to bring the ships back home. The German Naval War Command foresaw new tasks for the ships in attacking the Allied Murmansk convoys, while Hitler was primarily interested in securing Norway against any Allied raids or landings.

Breaking through the Channel seemed to offer better prospects of success than a voyage through the Atlantic to Norway via Iceland. The preparations were made under the greatest secrecy. Minesweepers spent weeks sweeping the route clear of mines in an attempt to veil the purpose of the coming operation. Six destroyers, fourteen torpedo boats and three S-boat flotillas were ordered into Channel ports so that they could guard the formation. One hundred and seventy-six fighter aircraft were made ready. In order to take the Allies by surprise it was planned to put to sea at night and break through by day.

The British had anticipated such an attempt, but expected it to be made at night. In fact, a coincidental series of technical breakdowns, missed sightings and the jamming of British radar apparatus prevented the German ships being detected until just before they reached the Dover Straits towards noon on 12 February 1942. A Spitfire spotter located them, but its report arrived too late to alert the coastal batteries at Dover. The photograph here shows the *Prinz Eugen* firing her heavy AA guns at Swordfish torpedo aircraft as they carried out an attack.

German cruiser *Prinz Eugen*.

(previous pages) *Scharnhorst* and *Gneisenau* (background), and escorts in the Channel.

(abpve) *Campbeltown* after ramming the St Nazaire lock gates.

The picture on the preceding pages shows the German formation during its Channel passage on 12 February 1942 in heavy seas and very hazy conditions. From left to right can be seen a torpedo boat of the 3rd T flotilla, the *Gneisenau*, a destroyer of the 5th Z flotilla, in the mist the *Scharnhorst*, on the right-hand edge a torpedo boat of the 5th T flotilla.

After the ships had passed the Dover Straits eight British motor torpedo boats put to sea from Dover and Ramsgate but were intercepted by the German guard vessels and were unable to attack the warships. Six Swordfish torpedo aircraft were launched, but they were all shot down by fighters and ships' AA guns, and the twenty-eight Beaufort torpedo aircraft of RAF Coastal Command and 242 aircraft sent by Bomber Command either failed to locate the formation or missed the ships with their bombs. Attacks by five World War I destroyers which had put to sea from Harwich also failed in the face of German defensive fire.

However, British aircraft had improvised a minelaying operation, and as the *Scharnhorst* made her way along the Dutch coast she was damaged by two mines, and the *Gneisenau* by one, though they were able to continue. The Channel breakthrough was perceived as a severe blow to the pride of the Royal Navy. It should not be forgotten that Bomber Command had dropped no less than 3,413 tons of bombs on the ships while they were lying at Brest, and had lost 127 aircraft in so doing. However, on the night of 26/27 February 1942 a bomb hit the forepart of the docked *Gneisenau* during an air attack on Kiel, causing severe damage and killing 116 crew. In January 1943 Hitler ordered the decommissioning of the heavy ships, and the planned re-fit of the *Gneisenau* with 15in guns was abandoned. The *Gneisenau* never sailed again.

After the *Tirpitz* and other heavy ships had moved to Norway (see page 80) the British Admiralty realised the acute danger of these ships breaking out into the Atlantic sea routes. The British therefore drew up a plan to destroy the only dock in France which the Tirpitz could use – the great lock of St Nazaire. The destroyer *Campbeltown* (ex

Buchanan) was one of the Allies' fifty formerly American vessels, and her funnels were modified so that she looked like a German torpedo boat. The ship was to make a surprise approach at night and ram the dock gate, while commandos landed by motor torpedo boats and motor launches were to destroy port installations and the U-boat base. The picture above shows the *Campbeltown*, which had run into heavy German defensive fire about half a mile short of its target, after ramming the dock gate on 28 March 1942. German soldiers entered the ship to examine it, but the built-in time-delay explosive charge killed many of them. The raid cost the lives of 397 British men, but achieved its purpose.

In the first six months of 1942 the British and American command staffs discussed the possibility of a landing in France (see page 121) in 1942 (Sledgehammer) or, at the latest, in 1943 (Roundup). Initially, the British demand for a landing in North Africa had prevailed, since it was considered highly unlikely that an invasion was possible in 1942. However, the command staffs were eager to gain experience for the invasion of France, which would be a much more difficult undertaking. The result was Operation Jubilee, a seaborne assault, planned to be held on 19 August 1942 near Dieppe on the Channel coast. Six thousand one hundred mostly Canadian troops embarked on nine infantry landing ships and were to be taken to the shore by landing boats. Aircraft and minesweepers would provide support in addition to eight destroyers of the Hunt class. During the approach a section of the landing fleet came into contact with a small German coastal convoy, with the result that the Germans were alerted to the operation very early. German coastal artillery and sections of the 302nd Infantry Division, supported by dive bombers, hurled themselves against the landing forces, and by midday they had re-embarked without reaching most of their targets; 1,179 men died, 891 wounded and 2,190 were taken prisoner. One destroyer and thirty-three landing boats together with all thirty tanks (below) and 106 aircraft were lost. The German losses amounted to 311 dead and missing, 280 wounded and 48 aircraft.

The attack on Dieppe confirmed the fears of the Chief of the Imperial General Staff, General Sir Alan Brooke, that a landing in France with inadequate forces was doomed to failure. At the same time, however, the bitter experience which the Allies gained in the operation was exploited in the development of more refined landing techniques, and in the preparations for the invasions in North Africa and France.

Until 1942 most German convoys had been brought through the Channel successfully with the help of escort forces consisting primarily of converted fishing vessels, but in 1943 the British Coastal Forces and the aircraft of RAF Coastal Command increasingly gained the upper hand. Radar location systems situated at coastal stations made it increasingly likely that motor torpedo boats, supported by motor gunboats and fighter-bombers, could attack the convoys, and German losses began to mount. More powerful torpedo boats would have been useful to the Germans, but they could only be spared to escort the most important convoys.

Increasing effort was also required on the part of the Germans to cope with the air mine offensive in the Channel off the Dutch coast and in the German Bight, most of which was carried out by RAF Bomber Command. Some of the German minesweepers were the larger Type 35 and 40s, of which a number had been built in Holland. Others were motor minesweepers, others again converted fishing vessels, but viewed overall they generally succeeded in clearing mine-free routes before the convoys.

For offensive operations on the German side the only boats available were the S-boats, most of which were sent out against allied convoys which had been located as a result of British radio traffic which had been overheard. However, improvements in weaponry and the installation of radar on convoy vessels made it increasingly difficult for the German vessels to carry out torpedo attacks, so reliance was placed increasingly on mines and mine operations.

Occasionally, battles took place in the Channel at night between the larger units. For example, on 23 October 1943 five German torpedo boats surprised an attacking British group and sank the cruiser *Charybdis* as well as the *Limbourne*, one of the seven destroyers taking part. On 26 and 29 April 1944 the German torpedo boats *T 29* and *T 27* were sunk together with the Canadian destroyer *Athabaskan* in similar skirmishes. Clashes between British motor gunboats or motor torpedo boats and the German S-boats or escort vessels, usually fought out at extremely close range in impossibly difficult situations, resulted in considerable losses on both sides.

Aftermath of the Dieppe raid.

German *Sperrbrecher 7* in the Bay of Biscay.

When the German U-boat bases were moved to France, securing the repair yards in the ports by building large U-boat pens became an urgent matter, and the British RAF Bomber Command failed to attack these installations while they were under construction. In early 1943 heavy attacks were carried out with the aim of wrecking the U-boat ports, but it was all too late; no U-boats were destroyed, and the civilian population suffered a large number of casualties.

The other factor which assumed tremendous importance in the success of the U-boat operations was the securing of the U-boats' routes in and out of the Bay of Biscay. The Allies made repeated attempts to use their own submarines to combat the German U-boats in this region, but in 1940 they had only two successes. The British therefore changed tactics and started intensive minelaying operations in the U-boat routes using high-speed minelayers and one French

mine submarine, but above all using British aircraft for the task. The mine offensive took on ever increasing significance from 1940 to 1944, and it could only be kept in check on the German side by thorough and sophisticated counter-measures. Freighters converted into barrage breakers (one of them, the *Sperrbrecher 7*, ex-*Sauerland*, is seen here on convoy duty in the Bay of Biscay) carried out mine convoy operations together with converted fishing trawlers and luggers which had been bequeathed to the Germans in French ports. In 1940 178 German and Italian submarines were directed in and out of port without loss. In 1941 there was a single loss from 637 boats, in 1942 two losses from 866, in 1943 one loss from 971 and in 1944 three losses from 420.

In July 1942 the 19th Group of RAF Coastal Command, operating from southwest England, began carrying out air attacks against the incoming and outgoing U-boats in

the Bay of Biscay. Until the end of the year the submarines generally managed to evade the attacks in good time by diving, although six U-boats were lost in these actions. However, the introduction of 9 cm radar and the installation of Leigh Light searchlights on some British aircraft caused a dramatic increase in losses in the first six months of 1943, the figure rising to fifteen submarines sunk. Experiments were carried out with U-boats arranged in groups for the Biscay crossing, so that the AA armament of all the boats together could be used to ward off aircraft, but the British responded to this by employing their aircraft en masse, and the net result was a further twenty-two losses and many seriously damaged U-boats by the end of the year.

The supply of scarce raw materials from East Asia, especially rubber, was extremely important to the success of Germany's war economy. In an effort to counter a developing shortage, the first five German and Italian high-speed motor freighters were sent to sea as blockade breakers in the winter months of

1940/41, travelling from Japan to France, with the idea of taking advantage of the longer nights. Three of these vessels reached Bordeaux successfully. In 1941/42 seven German ships put to sea from France for the return voyage, of which six made it to Japan, while nine of the twelve ships from Japan arrived safely in Bordeaux. Between August and December 1942 fifteen ships left Bordeaux and nine reached Japan. In the same period nine ships put to sea from Dairen, Yokohama and Kobe, but only two of them reached their destination. Two of these ships were captured in the Indian Ocean, but most of the problems arose when they tried to break through into the Bay of Biscay. To counter these losses four battle-worthy German destroyers steamed through the Channel to Bordeaux in the period 5 to 8 March 1943, with the intention of escorting the six blockade breakers on their way in to France, and secure the outward passage for four further freighters. However, one of the incoming ships was sunk by mistake by a German U-boat, two were captured by cruisers in the South Atlantic and the Denmark Straits, and two fell into the British net to the west of Biscay, outside the range of the destroyers. Only the Italian *Pietro Orseolo* was protected effectively by the destroyers against air attacks and brought in to Bordeaux, although the ship was damaged by an American submarine torpedo. Of the outgoing ships only two reached Japan.

In 1943/44 it was intended that a further five ships should sail to France from Japan. Although the Allies received indirect warnings of this plan by Ultra radio decrypts, the first two ships did reach Biscay. From there they were to be brought in by six German destroyers and fleet torpedo boats each, in two separate operations, but the operation was only successful with the *Osorno*. The *Alsterufer*, in contrast, was set on fire and sunk by a Czech-crewed bomber (see top right). On 28 December the destroyers which had put to sea into the Bay of Biscay were intercepted by the British cruisers *Glasgow* and *Enterprise*, and in heavy weather they sank the leading destroyer *Z 27* and the torpedo boats *T 25* and *T 26*. The photograph on the right shows two of the fleet torpedo boats shortly before the battle.

(top) German freighter *Alsterufer* on fire after air attack, Bay of Biscay.

(right) German torpedo-boats.

In this famous image we see infantrymen of the US 1st Division storming through chest-high water onto the Normandy 'Omaha' beaches near Vierville in the grey morning of 6 June 1944, having left an LCVP manned by the US Coast Guard.

The operation which began with scenes like this was the greatest amphibious operation yet attempted, but it had an extensive pre-history. At the Arcadia conference in Washington in December 1941 Roosevelt and Churchill decided that even after Japan had joined in the war it was essential to stick to the Europe first strategy which they had already agreed, in a bid to start with the most dangerous enemy, Germany, and wrestle her to the ground, now that she had established herself in what she termed Fortress Europe. The methods of fulfilling this ambition were the subject of continual differences of opinion between the American and British Chiefs of Staff.

In the spring of 1942 American tacticians examined the possibility of carrying out amphibious landings on all the coasts of Europe, and came to the conclusion that the only ones within range of land-based aircraft operations were those of northern France. It was only in northern France that the terrain allowed the possibility of decisive actions right into the heart of Germany, since there were mountains blocking the route from every other coast. They therefore recommended that landings should be made in France (Operation Roundup) in the spring or summer of 1943. To allow for the possibility of a crisis in Russia they also decided to plan Operation Sledgehammer for 1942, whose purpose was the seizure of the Cotentin peninsula.

The British considered it impracticable to build up a fighting force strong enough to oppose the German army in France until such time as a permanent victory over the U-boats had been achieved. However, they decided to make use of the available forces by carrying out the plan for Operation Torch in summer 1942 – the landing in North Africa. In so doing they initiated a Mediterranean strategy which led to the postponement of the landing in France until 1944 (see pages 120 to 130).

US troops land in Normandy.

The Chief of Staff of the US Army, General Marshall, who had been reluctant to agree to a postponement of Operation Roundup at the Casablanca conference in January 1943, did succeed in setting up a planning staff called Cossac whose purpose was to work out plans for a fast transfer of troops to Europe in the case of a German collapse (Operation Rankin). Cossac also laid plans for a large-scale offensive landing in France in 1944. The date of this Operation Neptune/Overlord was agreed at the Trident summit conference in May 1943, and was to be 1 May 1944.

The first task of Cossac was the choice of landing site. It had to lie within the range of fighter aircraft stationed in England. It also had to be blessed with suitable beaches and be within reach of at least one major port, with good prospects of capturing it. The army members of the planning staff preferred the region around the Pas de Calais as it offered the most direct route into the Ruhr region, but Admiral Lord Mountbatten as British Chief of Combined Operations made it clear that the coast of Normandy would provide better protection against the prevailing westerly winds, and the German defensive installations in that area were much less powerful than those at the Pas de Calais.

At the Quadrant conference in Quebec in August 1943 General Morgan, the Chief of Staff of Cossac, presented his plan. It foresaw the landing of three divisions in Normandy initially, followed by eight more, and the capture of Cherbourg within two weeks. A simultaneous landing was to take place in southern France. Churchill demanded that the landing force should be 25 per cent larger, and to meet this requirement additional landing vessels had to be assigned to the operation. These could be drawn from either of two sources: from the Mediterranean, which would require a postponement of the landing in southern France, or from the Pacific contingent. On 3 December 1943 Roosevelt appointed General Eisenhower Supreme Allied Commander.

The German Command expected the landing to take place in France in the spring of 1944, and had therefore strengthened the forces of the Commander-in-Chief West. They considered the most likely landing place to be the Pas de Calais, which fell within the 15th Army's sector, and gave Normandy and the 7th Army much less credence. Field Marshal Rommel, Commander-in-Chief of Army Group B, wanted his tank formations to be stationed as close as possible to the coast, in spite of the expected Allied aerial superiority, so that they could immediately be employed for counter-attacks against the bridgeheads which would form there. Other generals hoped that the landed forces could be hemmed in by divisions of tanks in open country.

The Allies set up a large-scale, long-term radio 'game' of deception, and succeeded in convincing German intelligence that they were preparing the 1st US Army Group, which actually did not exist, in southeast England for a planned landing at the Pas de Calais. The purpose of the deception was to tie down the forces of the German 15th Army in that area, and that is exactly what they managed to do.

British monitor *Roberts* and (background) cruiser *Frobisher*.

British troops landing on 'Juno' beach.

During the night of 6 June 1944, after continuous air attacks employing 3,467 heavy bombers and 1,645 medium and light bombers under the protection of 5,409 fighters, two US airborne divisions were landed from 2,316 transport aircraft in the south of the Cotentin peninsula, while one British parachute division was landed southeast of Caen. They were followed from the sea in the grey of the early morning by troops, landing on five sections of beach which had each been assigned a cover name: the 4th US division on the east coast of the Cotentin peninsula (Utah), the 1st US Division near Vierville (Omaha) and the 50th British, 3rd Canadian and 3rd British Divisions near Arromanches (Gold), Courseulles (Juno) and Lyon-sur-Mer (Sword). By the evening of 6 June

109,715 men had been landed. The photograph above shows units of the British 3rd Division landing with bicycles from LCIs in the Juno area near Bernieres station to the north of Caen, before advancing inland to the 6th Airborne Division which had been dropped inland from the air.

Artillery support from the sea was of particular significance in the first phase of Operation Neptune. In the picture on the left the British monitor *Roberts* is seen firing its 15in guns at a German coastal battery near Houlgate. In the background can be seen the British cruiser *Frobisher*. The coastal bombardment was carried out by five battleships, two monitors, twenty cruisers, two gunboats and forty-five destroyers from six navies. A total of 204 minesweepers and 43 buoy-layers

took part in the landings in the five areas, seeking out and marking the approach routes, together with five command ships, 55 large transports, 236 tank landing ships (LST) and 2,484 medium and smaller landing and auxiliary vessels. Twenty-three American, forty-nine British, three French, three Polish, two Norwegian and two Dutch ships provided artillery support. By 12 June sixteen divisions had been landed by air and sea, with a total of 326,000 men, 54,000 vehicles and 104,000 tons of supplies. The losses amounted to about 2,500 dead and 8,500 wounded.

Survivors from mined Allied ships off 'Omaha' beach.

The German LXXXIV Corps was assigned the task of warding off a landing in Normandy and the Cotentin peninsula, with one airborne, two infantry and two static defence divisions, with more than forty-three infantry battalions and twelve artillery battalions available. Only part of this force was accommodated in fortified or bunkered positions. They were supported by a number of army and naval coastal batteries with calibres ranging from 4in to 6½in, some of them French prize guns commandeered in 1940. Only the Marcouf battery by the Utah beach sector had 8in guns, and it had three of them, even though they also were only partially bunkered. Beach obstacles, like those visible in the photograph opposite, were intended to make landings more difficult, but they had relatively little effect. All the force the German Luftwaffe could muster was eighty-

eight bombers, 159 fighter-bombers and spotters and 172 fighters. Apart from the auxiliary escort vessels, which could not be expected to offer defence against an invasion fleet, the Germans' serviceable naval force consisted of three destroyers and five torpedo boats at Brest and Le Havre, thirty-four S-boats at Ostende, Boulogne, Le Havre and Cherbourg, and thirty-seven U-boats, nine of them equipped with snorkels, standing by in their bases in the Bay of Biscay. Extensive mine blockades had been laid off the coast, but in the first few days of the invasion neither the Luftwaffe nor the ships and U-boats were able to make much impact against the powerful protective forces of the invasion fleet, and they failed to achieve any successes of note.

On the Allied side the greatest difficulties arose on 6 June 1944 at the Omaha

breachead, as shown in the photograph on the right. At this point the invaders met the battle-ready 352nd Division and were only able to hold a narrow bridgehead, with the loss of 3,000 dead and wounded. A large part of the losses was due to damage to landing boats and amphibious tanks when they ran onto beach obstacles and subsequently flooded. The water was more than head-high, and many soldiers sank, unable to keep themselves afloat with the burden of their heavy equipment, although US Coast Guard cutters often succeeded in rescuing men under heavy German gunfire, eventually saving around 1,500 men from the water, amongst them sailors from ships which had run onto German mines. The picture above was taken from one of these cutters, and shows sailors swimming in the water and another vessel in the background coming to their aid.

The picture below shows a section of the Omaha beach towards the evening of 6 June: on the beach dead soldiers, wrecked lorries and a Sherman tank, behind them the beach obstacles, on the left a beached American LST, in the background transport vessels and between them and the beach landing craft plying to and fro.

In the British sector the sole German tank division set off from Caen on 6 June, advanced between the beach areas Sword and Juno and reached the coast, but was forced to withdraw under the onslaught of the ships' guns. In the following few days German reinforcements approached, although their progress was much delayed by carefully targeted attacks by the Allied air forces on their approach routes. The Germans were unable to prevent the Allied bridgeheads joining up, and by 12 June they formed a secure landing area over 50 miles wide and 5 to 20 miles deep. It was virtually impossible for the Germans to make any inroads into this landing space, since it was now so broad.

Every night and all night long over the period 6 to 15 June, the four German torpedo boats from Le Havre and the S-boats from Ostende and Boulogne belonging to the 4th and 5th Flotillas tried to penetrate into the landing area, but they only succeeded in sinking the Norwegian destroyer *Svenner* and, later, two LSTs, while the S-boats of the 9th Flotilla operating out of Cherbourg sank two LSTs and two smaller landing boats. The Germans also suffered many losses and much damage night after night. The three destroyers and one fleet torpedo boat from Brest, which tried to reach the invasion area on 8/9th June, were intercepted by four British, two Canadian and two Polish destroyers and two of the ships were lost. However, the heaviest loss of shipping was due to mines, and was suffered by the Allies. By the end of June eleven ships had been sunk by mines altogether, amongst them six destroyers and two minesweepers, and twenty-three ships had been damaged.

Of the thirty-six German U-boats belonging to the Landwirt group, which had put to sea from Brest, St Nazaire, La Pallice and Lorient, only nine were equipped with a snorkel. By 9 June four of the non snorkel-equipped boats had been sunk and six severely damaged by allied aircraft, with the result that the U-boats without snorkels had to be withdrawn, since they had no chance of penetrating into the Channel. The Allies had anticipated the appearance of the snorkel-equipped U-boats, and had prepared six British and four Canadian Support Groups, consisting of three escort carriers, fourteen destroyers and forty frigates, off the western entrance to the Channel, of which six were always at sea. Of the nine snorkel-equipped U-boats based in France four were completely unsuccessful against these Support Groups, and three of the submarines were lost. It was not until 15 June 1944 that three German U-boats reached the invasion area and sank two frigates and one landing ship. On 29 June *U 984* managed the U-boats only major success when she torpedoed four transports.

'Omaha' beach.

Since the Allies could not expect to capture a major port quickly and in an undamaged state, they had planned to construct two artificial installations known as Mulberry harbours. As early as 7 June 1944 the first ones were assembled at the Omaha beach and in the British Gold sector near Arromanches. The first step was to sink fifty-three old merchant ships and warships ('gooseberries'), to form breakwaters, amongst them the old

British battleship *Centurion*, the old French battleship *Courbet*, the Dutch cruiser *Sumatra* and the Polish cruiser *Durban*. These were supplemented by floating steel rafts called bombardons and massive sinking structures, which were termed Phœnix. Inside these breakwaters mooring points were anchored to secure large and smaller ships. Floating steel pontoon bridges designated whales were also laid out so that vehi-

cles and tanks from landing ships could land directly on them and run through the shallow water to the beach. Steel nets were laid on the beaches to reinforce the roads.

The photograph above shows the construction of the artificial ports on the Omaha beach sector, with transports in the background moored to the sunken 'gooseberry' freighters, and a pontoon ferry on the left. In the foreground LSTs are aground in the pletely destroyed Mulberry A harbour at Omaha beach and had driven about eight hundred landing craft and ferries ashore. The harbour at Arromanches was better sheltered by cliffs and was under the lee of the Le Havre peninsula, and so was able to resume activities on 21 June. It had been planned to land about 22,570 tons of supplies per day, but during the gale days only about 3,400 tons had reached land each day. This eventuality caused a supply crisis, although the Germans failed to realise the Allied difficulty, and did not exploit the situation by carrying out a general counter-attack. The aerial photograph below shows the Mulberry B harbour off Aromanches with the bombardon breakwaters at the front, the north entrance on the left, four Liberty ships, and the floating pontoon bridges running out from the beach to the piers for mooring supply vessels and landing vessels.

On 22 June thirteen more troop transports, thirty-eight tank landing ships of the LST type (Landing Ship Tank) and thirty coastal ships arrived, followed by 165 of the smaller LCT landing craft (Landing Craft Tank) and fourteen LCIs (Landing Craft Infantry) on the twenty-third. By the end of June a total of 180 troop transports, 570 Liberty ships, 788 coastal ships, 905 LSTs, 1,442 LCTs and 372 LCIs had unloaded their cargoes: 861,838 men, 157,633 vehicles and 501,843 tons of supplies.

The storm and the loss of the Mulberry A harbour made the capture of Cherbourg an even more urgent necessity. The US VI Corps, which had cut off the overland route to Cherbourg on 18 June, attacked the tightly enclosed fortification on 22 June, and on 27 June forced it to surrender after heavy artillery support by the battleships *Nevada*, *Texas* and *Arkansas*, together with the cruisers *Quincy*, *Tuscaloosa*, *Glasgow* and *Enterprise*.

By this time the strategic bombers placed at Eisenhower's disposal for the period of the invasion had eliminated the German surface ships at Le Havre and Boulogne in two heavy raids.

(left) 'Omaha' beach, D-Day + 1.

(below) 'Mulberry-B' harbour off Arromanches, late June 1944.

shallow water, in the front an Amtrack amphibious vehicle and steel net tracks laid out.

Although storms are rare in the Channel in June, the barometer began to fall very quickly on 18 June 1944. On the 19 a northeasterly gale blew up, and the landing of troops and supplies soon had to be halted as a result. The storm raged undiminished until 21 June, by which time it had almost com-

German prisoners take a wounded comrade to an evacuation craft.

The Allied attacks on the bridgehead encountered stiff German resistance and gained ground at a slow rate, so RAF Bomber Command and the strategic 8th US Air Fleet were now brought in to help the army troops force a breakthrough into the German positions by laying concentrated 'carpets' of bombs. Two operations in the British 2nd Army's sector on 8 and 17 July 1944 resulted in the capture of Caen, but the advance then became bogged down again. The way out of the bridgehead was only opened up by an operation in which 4,200 tons of bombs were dropped on an area 1.5 by 3.5 miles to the west of St. Lo, allowing the US VII Corps through on 25 July. On 31 July the Americans reached Avranches and in the next few days stormed into Brittany and on in the direction of Le Mans. Hitler ordered a counter-attack near Mortain on 6 August, but the Allies' Signal Intelligence picked up the plan in good time and foiled it. This led to the surrounding of a large part of the 7th Army and of the 5th Tank Army near Falaise. Isolated sections managed to break out of the 'kettle', but 45,000 Germans were taken prisoner.

This brought to an end the greatest amphibious operation in history. It had resulted in great losses on both sides: by 23 July the Allies could count 122,000 dead, wounded and missing, the Germans around 117,000. By the end of the battle for the 'kettle' of Falaise the German losses had risen to around 400,000 men including those taken prisoner.

In the photograph above German prisoners can be seen carrying a severely wounded comrade past newly landed American soldiers to a landing craft which would take them to ships lying off the coast for treatment.

Between 25 August and mid-September 1944 the German troops pulled back to the Westwall, the Albert canal and the Schelde estuary, and the front eventually came to a halt at Maas and Niederrhein after the British failed to break through at Arnhem on 22 September, and after the evacuation and flooding of the island of Walcheren by the Germans before the Allies landed there on 1 November. The Germans had ships lying in Dutch yards which they tried to bring to safety by running convoys to German ports before the Allies arrived. These convoys became the target of attacks by RAF Coastal Command's Mosquito bombers and Beaufighter torpedo aircraft, and they sank eighty-eight German ships, new vessels under tow, auxiliary warships, fast boats and armaments between September 1944 and April 1945 along the Dutch coast and the southern North Sea. Over six thousand missions were flown, and sixty-nine of the allied aircraft were lost in the operations. Numerous other ships and vessels were damaged, and many German sailors lost their lives. Pictured below are British Beaufighters of Squadrons 143, 236 and 254 attacking German patrol boats off Heligoland on 17 September 1944. The boat *V 1201* was sunk and *V 1202* was severely damaged, later sinking after striking a mine.

On the German side S-boats were dispatched repeatedly in the period autumn 1944 to spring 1945 in attempts to approach allied shipping off the southeast coast of England, but their successes were few and far between, and considerable losses were sustained. Eventually, their bases were destroyed by Allied bombers, and their missions were brought to a halt.

RAF Beaufighters attack German patrol boats off Heligoland.

Battle of the Atlantic IV

25 May 1943–8 May 1945

In early May 1943 the greatest number of U-boats ever employed against a single convoy was sent to attack convoy ONS.5, and six of the submarines were sunk. In the following two double operations against convoys HX.237 / SC.129 and HX.239 / SC.130 the German U-boat formations did not succeed in approaching the convoys, now covered by support groups and with thorough air protection, in spite of outstanding help from the radio decoding of the xB-Dienst. The U-boat losses had been relatively steady at fourteen, thirteen and twelve per month, but they suddenly rose to thirty-one, prompting the Commander of the U-boats to call off the fight against the North Atlantic convoys on 24 May. Instead, the U-boats were transferred to the USA-Gibraltar route and more distant regions with weaker defensive measures, where they had a better chance of survival. This change involved sending the available U-boat tankers out to mid-Atlantic. In early June *U 488* was able to re-fuel the fourteen U-boats of the Trutz group in the Azores region, and subsequently eight other returning submarines, but the large minelaying U-boat *U 118*, operating as an auxiliary supply vessel, was attacked by eight aircraft from the US escort carrier *Bogue* on 12 June (as shown in the picture below) and sunk.

Ultra decryption had allowed the British to detect the U-boat evacuation of the North Atlantic and the establishment of the Trutz group, and this information in turn gave them the opportunity to divert the USA-Gibraltar convoys. However, in July 1943 individual U-boats operating alone in distant regions achieved a number of successes, and the Ultra system was unable to prevent them. The picture on the right shows survivors from a British freighter sunk by a German U-boat being rescued by a US Coast Guard cutter.

(below) U 118 under air attack.

(right) Crew of British freighter rescued by US Coast Guard.

In July 1943 the number of newly-built merchant ships for the first time exceeded the number of ships sunk. More and more of the Liberty ships mass-produced in the USA crossed the North Atlantic in huge convoys, as shown in the photograph above. From the end of May to mid-September 1943 the threat to the convoys from U-boats was virtually negligible, since they had shifted their operational region into the mid-Atlantic, the African coasts and the Central American and South American coasts. In the mid-Atlantic American Hunter-Killer groups operated in support of the USA-Gibraltar convoys. Each of these groups consisted of one escort carrier and three to five destroyers, and they made life difficult for the U-boat tankers waiting for the U-boats arriving in and leaving the area. Once a U-boat had been detected, it was hunted relentlessly. In the picture on the left a US destroyer launches a depth charge against a U-boat. On the right another lays a carpet of depth charges on a submerged U-boat after having been directed to the location by a Catalina flying-boat based in Morocco.

(top) 'Liberty ships' in convoy, July 1943.
(left) US destroyer firing depth-charge.

(above) Destroyer depth-charging U-boat located by Catalina.

(above) British escort carrier.

(right) US escort destroyer *Liddle*, May 1944.

At the Casablanca conference in January 1943 Churchill and Roosevelt and their respective Chiefs of Staff had placed the defeat of the U-boats at the top of their list of priorities. In early March the Atlantic conference of the American, British and Canadian staffs concerned had agreed that the most important requirement in this project was the closure of the 'air gap' over the North Atlantic by assigning Very Long Range (VLR) Liberators to the task. By May 1943 one squadron based in Northern Ireland had been equipped with fifteen of these machines, another in Iceland and another in Newfoundland. They had a decisive part to play in the turning of the tide in May 1943.

A further agreed requirement was the formation of Support Groups, each of which was to consist of one escort carrier and three to five destroyers. By the end of 1942 nine-

teen escort carriers had already been completed in the USA, seven of which were transferred to the Royal Navy together with another built in England, but it was not until the end of March and May 1943 respectively that the *Bogue* and HMS *Archer* arrived in the North Atlantic. It was the end of May 1943 before the first five Support Groups, mostly consisting of four to five destroyers on their own, were helping to push the convoys through the U-boat formations of which they were forewarned in location and number by the Ultra radio decrypts. The British escort carriers were initially equipped with nine Swordfish aircraft for U-boat attack and three Martlet fighters, although later they received more modern aircraft such as Avengers for U-boat hunting and Wildcat or Hellcat fighters, as can be spotted in the photograph above.

In 1943 the Support Groups centred around British escort carriers usually consisted of fleet destroyers detached from the Home Fleet, but the American Hunter-Killer groups which started to operate in mid-

Atlantic in July 1943 were being steadily equipped with new escort destroyers to replace the old World War I destroyers. The picture on the right shows the US Buckley class escort destroyer *Liddle* in May 1944. These 1,400-ton ships had turbo-electric propulsion and were armed with three 3in guns, one 1.1in quad and eight 20mm guns plus a triple torpedo tube system. They possessed radar, sonar and HF/DF location apparatus, eight depth charge launchers and two depth charge rails at the stern for combatting U-boats. These are clearly visible in the photograph, as are the Hedgehog launchers forward of the bridge. The Royal Navy also took delivery of similar ships, and they were used as the basis for new Escort Groups which were formed in late 1943.

The most effective U-boat hunter vessels apart from destroyers, corvettes and frigates were the sloops which constituted the most successful 2nd Escort Group amongst others.

The German U-boat Command hoped to be able to regain the upper hand in convoy fighting in the North Atlantic which they had lost in May 1943 by introducing more modern weapons. Until such time as they were ready, they planned to employ the U-boats in regions where the defensive measures were less sophisticated.

The Indian Ocean appeared to offer potential in this respect, particularly since a group of six large Type IXD2 boats had sunk thirty-two ships in the region around Madagascar. The submarines were supplied by one tanker based in the Japanese base of Penang.

In December 1942 the Japanese had expressed a desire for nine Type IXC boats and one U-boat tanker to pass through the northern Indian Ocean and operate out of Penang, and July 1943 was set as the time for the plans implementation. However, on the voyage east three U-boats were sunk by Allied aircraft in the region of the Azores, and the U-boat tanker had to return after

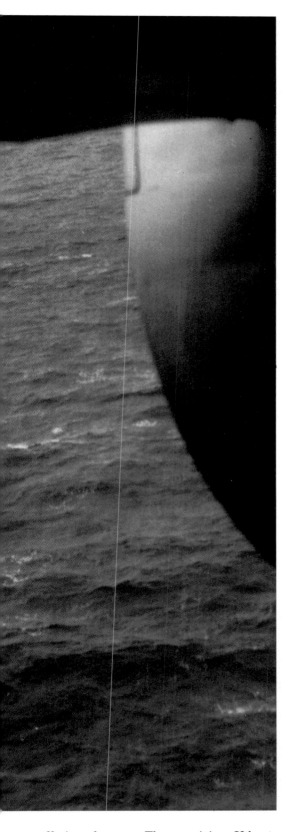

tem had also been introduced there, with the result that by the end of September they had only succeeded in sinking six ships and six dhows.

In the meantime the US Atlantic Fleet had introduced aircraft in an effort to improve its monitoring of the Freetown – Natal Straits in the South Atlantic. These aircraft operated from bases in Brazil and the island of Ascension, and were employed to support the ships of the 4th Fleet. Of the Type IXD2 boats which followed the Monsun group, *U 848* was attacked and sunk on 5 November 1943 southwest of the island of Ascension by four Liberator bombers which had taken off from the island, and two army bombers which were en route for Africa.

The photograph on the left was taken from one of the aircraft, and shows the impact of the aircraft's shells and a depth charge exploding adjacent to the boat. *U 849* followed, and suffered a similar fate on 25 November, while *U 850* was sunk by five car-

(left) U 848 under attack by US bombers.

(below) U 604 hit by depth-charge from a Ventura bomber, 30/7/43.

rier aircraft from the *Bogue* on 20 December. One hundred and ninety-two men were lost when the submarines sank.

The nine German U-boats sent out to operate along the Brazilian coast in July 1943 sank five convoy ships and thirteen lone vessels as well as two sailing boats. However, in July alone five of the U-boats were destroyed by American and Brazilian aircraft. *U 604* suffered an unusual fate: on 30 July it suffered serious damage from depth charges dropped by a Ventura bomber which was guarding the Brazilian convoy TJ.2, as portrayed in the photograph below. The commander of the U-boat radioed a request for help, and it was planned that *U 185* and *U 172* should rendezvous on 3 August, but the Americans decrypted the radio signal. A Liberator from Ascension duly attacked and damaged *U 185*, while the destroyer *Moffett* caused severe damage to *U 604* with depth charges and gunfire. A new rendezvous planned for 11 August was again decrypted, and while the crew of the scuttled *U 604* was transferring to *U 185* the same Liberator attacked, but was itself shot down by the submarine. Finally, on 24 August, American carrier aircraft sank *U 185*. Two hundred and eighty-nine men of eight crews died, and eighty-four were captured.

suffering damage. The surviving U-boats then had to be supplied by improvised means in the area between the Azores and Cape Verdes, leading to further losses through American Hunter-Killer groups. For this reason only five of the Type IXC U-boats of the Monsun group finally reached the Indian Ocean, although by this time the convoy sys-

U-boat pen at a base in France.

The photograph here was taken in November 1943 and shows a view inside one of the concrete bunkers built at French bases to protect U-boats against Allied air attacks. Starting in June 1943 the German U-boat Command fitted out their boats with the new Hagenuk Wanz radio measurement observation apparatus, and more powerful AA armament consisting of a 20mm quad and two 20mm twins, together with the new Zaunkönig homing torpedoes. With the submarines so equipped, U-boat Command hoped to be able to resume convoy fighting in the autumn. The Leuthen group put to sea in late August with a total of twenty U-boats,

and to their surprise they passed through the Bay of Biscay into the Atlantic without loss. In September they were re-fuelled in mid-ocean, then deployed in a formation across the route of the expected convoys ON.202 and ONS.18. On this occasion Ultra decrypted messages arrived too late to give the convoys a chance of escaping. Allied air protection in mid-Atlantic was relatively weak at this time because the aircraft were concentrated in the Biscay region, and as a result twelve boats were able to approach the convoys and carry out twenty-four attacks using the Zaunkönig torpedo. They claimed to have sunk twelve destroyers and torpedoed seven merchant ships. However, the German reports of successful attacks were again decrypted, and provided information to

the Allies which proved to be important in combatting these new weapons. On the German side the successes were considerably over-estimated because numerous torpedoes exploded when they struck ship wakes, or reach the limit of their range. In fact only four escorts and seven steamers had been hit. U-boat Command was eager to exploit the supposed success of their new weapons, and began forming U-boat groups for the next attack, but the Allies countered this move by sending their long-range aircraft and Support Groups back onto the convoy routes. The escorts were fitted with Foxer and Cat sound generators developed to thwart the target-seeking torpedoes which worked on acoustic principles.

In October and November 1943 the Ultra decrypts became available earlier and earlier thanks to the introduction of the American so-called 'High Speed Bombs', with the result that it was possible to dispatch additional air and sea protection to cover endangered convoys. In consequence all attempts by U-boat Command to resume successful operations against the North Atlantic convoys were doomed to failure, and on 7 November Dönitz was once again obliged to break off the operations. Now his only recourse was to adopt a delaying tactic by carrying out attacks using the old U-boats, in an attempt to tie down the Allied forces until the new U-boats currently under construction were ready for active service. Revolutionary Walter U-boats were under development but could not be completed in time, so all the Germans' efforts were concentrated on the sectional building of the fast electric boats of the large Type XXI and the small Type XXIII, of which 190 and 110 respectively were ordered. The Type XXI boats, with their hydrodynamically optimised hull form, increased battery capacity and more powerful electric motors, were designed to have a top speed when submerged of 16 knots, which would enable them to escape from most escort vessels. They were fitted with active location apparatus and could fire three fans of six torpedoes within a short period thanks to their rapid loading systems. It was essential that the boats should be able to recharge their batteries under water by running the diesel engines, which required an air supply. To meet this requirement the submarines were fitted with a snorkel air mast, the head of which remained above the surface when the boat was submerged, as shown in the picture on the right. In the top photograph we see *U 2501*, the first Type XXI boat, after launching at the Blohm & Voss yard in Hamburg on 12 May 1944.

The Allies learned of this new boat and its characteristics from decrypted reports which the Japanese embassy in Berlin radioed to Tokyo. In late 1944 decrypted Ultra messages and air reconnaissance indicated that quite a large number of these boats were in commission and the Allies grew very anxious about an entirely new U-boat war, against which as yet no defensive measures were available. However, although 104 boats had been completed by May 1945, the Allied air offensive against the transport routes and the advance of the Allied armies from East and West prevented them being made ready for the front.

(below) First Type XXI U-boat, *U 2501*, after launch.
(bottom) A Snorkel.

U 505 captured by US ships.

From mid-1944 onward the old Type VII and IX boats had been modified to take a snorkel, so that they could operate continuously while submerged, and these vessels now had to bear the burden of the delaying operation. This operation was designed to provide up-to-date information and experience on convoy organisation prior to the resumption of convoy fighting when the new boats arrived, and also to keep Allied forces busy combatting U-boats so that they could not be employed in any other way.

The photograph here shows *U 505* on 4 June 1944 after being forced to surface by a

US Hunter-Killer group which included the escort carrier *Guadalcanal*. The crew is about to disembark before a prize crew from the destroyer *Pillsbury* moves in. Their task was to prevent the submarine sinking. The boat was subsequently towed to America and proved to be a comprehensive source of useful information, especially in terms of radio intelligence. It was eventually set up as a museum in Chicago where it can be viewed to this day.

In the final year of the war snorkel-

equipped U-boats carried out approximately 400 attack operations in which they sank or torpedoed forty-seven convoy vessels and 173 merchant ships; 194 U-boats were lost during this time.

The number of sailors who lost their lives in the U-boat war is quite shocking. Around 41,000 men were employed in front-line U-boats on active service, and of them 26,350 died fighting the enemy, 947 died as a result of accidents, 4,945 were taken prisoner and only 2,459 were rescued.

The Baltic and the North Sea

1 September 1944–8 May 1945

In January 1944 the Soviet offensive began against the German ring enclosing Leningrad. In this operation all available battleships – including the *Oktyabrskaya Revolutsiya* shown in the picture on the right – cruisers, destroyers and gunboats were put into action, firing a total of 24,000 shells in support of the 2nd Shock Army which was attacking from the Oranienbaum bridgehead. When the Soviets broke through into the Riga Sea Bay in early August 1944, the Germans also brought up their heavy ships to support their hard-pressed army troops, amongst them the cruiser *Admiral Hipper* pictured below.

(above) Soviet battleship *Oktyabrskaya Revolutsiya* at Leningrad.

(below) German heavy cruiser *Admiral Hipper*.

(*above and left*) Refugees fleeing the Russians in Baltic ports.

Finland's involvement in the war ceased on 4 September 1944. With this, and the failure of the German attempt to secure the mine and net barrages in the Bay of Finland by occupying Suursaari, the German Command decided to evacuate Estland by sea. By 23 September 50,000 soldiers and 85,000 refugees had been evacuated via Reval. On 10 October the Soviets broke through into the Baltic to the south of Libau and cut off Army Group North at the Kurland bridgehead. Freighters carrying supplies from Germany were loaded with refugees for the return voyage, as shown in the photograph above, taken at Windau in October 1944. The first major loss in this operation was the sinking of the *Bremerhaven* by Soviet aircraft on 31 October, in which 410 people died. After the Soviet landings on Dagoe and Oesel, German cruisers, destroyers and torpedo boats supported the defenders of the Sworbe peninsula with artillery fire.

On 12 January 1945 the great offensive by the Soviet armies began on the Weichsel front, and in a few days they broke through the German positions. By the end of January the attacking forces had reached Silesia and the river Oder near Küstrin, and had cut off the German troops stationed in East Prussia by means of a push into the Kurisches Haff. Vast rivers of people fleeing the approaching Red Army flowed down to the coast, to the ports of Memel, Konigsberg, Pillau, Danzig and Gotenhafen (Gdingen), which were bitterly defended by the troops stationed there. In the second half of February the Soviet and Polish armies of Pomerania, which had broken through at the river Oder, attacked from the south. Once again they soon reached the coast, and only Kolbert was able to hold out.

On 25 January the greatest ever evacuation operation by sea began. All types of vessel from large passenger steamers to small private motor boats were loaded to their absolute limits with refugees, army units and wounded people. Warships steaming westward to pick up supplies after completing their troop support task also embarked as many as they could. The photograph at the bottom of the opposite page shows refugees crowding onto a passenger steamer moored to a pier, ready to cast off. In the picture below, taken in Gotenhafen (Gdingen) in January 1945, soldiers load goods onto a freighter for the return voyage. When the ships were at sea in the Bay of Danzig they had to survive attacks by Soviet bombers and attack aircraft, and after April attacks by

fast attack craft too. However, the greatest loss of life occurred when the large transports *Wilhelm Gustloff* and *General Steuben* were sunk by the Soviet submarine *S 13* on 30 January and 10 February 1945 respectively, and when the *Goya* was sunk by *L 3* on 16 April. Of the 16,678 people on the ships only 1,029 were rescued. These amounted to the greatest maritime disasters of all time. The total number of deaths was almost ten times as great as in the sinking of the *Titanic* in 1912, which was, until then, generally considered to be the worst sea accident ever. Overall 2,401,387 people were evacuated to the west via the Baltic in 1944 and 1945, of whom 33,082 died. Of the 1,081 ships which put to sea, 245 were lost.

German evacuation of Gotenhafen.

The greatest losses in shipping in the Baltic were caused by the mining of the essential southern Baltic routes which was carried out by British aircraft. In the period from January to March 1945 3,220 mines were laid, and they sank a total of sixty-seven ships. It took the greatest effort by German barrage breakers, minesweepers and guard boats to keep the essential routes clear of the bottom mines which were fitted with magnetic and acoustic detonators. The fact that they did not suffer even greater losses after October 1944, when Soviet submarines were operating in the open Baltic, was due in part to the submarines' need to stay outside the 20m depth line precisely to avoid the mine hazard, whereas the vast majority of transports were obliged to follow the shallow water routes. In the same way a small number of transports, destroyers and torpedo boats were able to make two voyages during the last few nights of the war, from 3 to 9 May 1945, thereby transporting a further 81,000 of the 150,000 persons waiting on Hela without loss.

Air attacks on the ports by RAF Bomber Command and the 8th US Army Air Force

also caused severe losses, and the intensity of the bombing raids had already increased greatly before the strategic bomber forces of Operation Overlord started their action on 16 September 1944. In one attack on Kiel by Bomber Command on the night of 23/24 July, 612 aircraft dropped 2,916 tons of bombs, and the passenger steamer *General Osorio*, which was in use as a residential vessel, was struck by several bombs, burned out and sank in the navy arsenal (see below). These attacks were increasingly targeted at supply industries, section yards, inland shipping routes and the dockyards in Bremen, Hamburg and Kiel where the new U-boats were under construction. In the period 1 August 1944 to 4 May 1945 47,429 tons of bombs were dropped on German ports in 15,424 raids, during which 115 aircraft were lost. One hundred and fifteen ships of all sizes were destroyed, together with thirty-nine completed and incomplete U-boats.

Particularly severe damage resulted from attacks by the 8th US Air Force on 31 December 1944 and 17 January 1945 on the Blohm & Voss yard in Hamburg, and on 30 March on Wilhelmshaven, Bremen and

Hamburg, in which nine Type XXI U-boats were destroyed amongst many other vessels. An attack by Bomber Command on the Deschimag yard in Bremen on the night of 21/22 February destroyed two Type XXI boats on the stocks, and these prevented the launch of a further four boats then being completed. In the top picture opposite, taken on 28 April 1945, a British soldier looks down at the construction installation at Deschimag and the bombed and jammed U-boats, after the British had occupied the yard.

After Hitler's suicide in Berlin, Grand Admiral Dönitz, whom Hitler had nominated President of the Reich, tried to have many of the refugees from the Bay of Danzig and Kurland transported to the West by sea before the war, now acknowledged as lost, came to its inevitable end. On 4 May the surrender of the units stationed in Holland and northwest Germany was signed in front of Field Marshal Montgomery. In contravention of the surrender terms many U-boat crews subsequently carried out the earlier Regenbogen command and scuttled their boats. All vessels at sea were ordered to fly a black flag and surrender to Allied ships. The

German accommodation ship *General Osorio* sunk at Kiel, July 1944.

(above) U-boat yards after capture by the British.

(left) [left to right] Speer, Dönitz and Jodl after capture.

U-boats lying in Germany and Norway were transferred to England over the following few weeks. The German surrender was signed in General Eisenhower's headquarters in Reims and confirmed at Karlshorst in the presence of the Russians, and this brought the fighting in Europe to an end on the morning of 8 May 1945.

On 23 May the last government of the Reich was taken prisoner at their final seat: the Naval Academy at Flensburg-Mürwik. The picture on the left shows Dönitz in the centre, Reichsminister Speer on the left and General Jodl on the right in the courtyard of the Flensburg police presidium after their capture.

War in the Pacific III
1 October 1943–2 September 1945

After their retreat from Guadalcanal and the Papua peninsula the Japanese were determined to hold the central Solomons and the region around the Huon Gulf as outposts for their main base at Rabaul, the principal town of the formerly German Bismarck archipelago. In April 1943 the Chief of the Combined Fleet, Admiral Yamamoto, flew to the Rabaul area to visit the troops. Informed by radio intelligence about his plans for travelling, the Americans sent out long-range fighters to intercept his aircraft, and on 18 April he was shot down. Yamamoto died and was succeeded by Admiral Koga.

On the Allied side General MacArthur was in command of the forces operating in the southwest Pacific, while the mobile fleet units remained under the control of the Pacific Fleet and its commander, Admiral Nimitz. In March 1943 it was decided that MacArthur's American-Australian forces should push forward through the Huon Gulf along the east coast of New Guinea to western New Britain, while sections of the Pacific Fleet under Admiral Halsey would steam to Bougainville, the western-most Solomon island, via the central Solomons. In the summer of 1943 Halsey started to put this plan into action by capturing air bases on New Georgia in a series of amphibious operations which resulted in repeated sea skirmishes at night, with considerable losses on both sides. In June MacArthur advanced to Salamaua and in September to Lae and Finschhafen on the Huon gulf. In so doing he gained the starting point required for an attack on the inner defensive ring of Rabaul. On 1 November 1943 the reinforced 3rd Marine Division landed in Empress Augusta Bay on Bougainville and formed a bridgehead there. The photograph here shows landing boats from the transport *President Jackson* en route to Empress Augusta Bay. On 26 December men of the 1st Marine Division waded from their landing craft onto the beaches of New Britain near Cape Gloucester, portrayed in the picture opposite.

It was not the purpose of the Americans to conquer large islands, but to build airfields in the bridgeheads which they created. From these airfields Rabaul could be suppressed.

(below) Landing craft off Bougainville.

(right) US Marines landing at Cape Gloucester.

The Japanese immediately responded to the landing in Empress Augusta Bay. The following night the two heavy cruisers, two light cruisers and six destroyers which were stationed at Rabaul attempted to attack the landing fleet, but they were intercepted by a US task group consisting of four new light cruisers and six destroyers, and were forced to turn back by radar-guided gunfire. The Japanese also dispatched aircraft from Truk and a formation of seven heavy cruisers and supply vessels to Rabaul.

At the time Admiral Halsey learned of this, on 4 November 1943, he had no heavy ships available with which to withstand the Japanese, as they were all at the Gilbert Islands in readiness for the planned landings.

The only large units were the two aircraft carriers *Saratoga* and *Princeton*, at that time shipping supplies at New Georgia, and they were immediately sent to attack the Japanese ships at Rabaul. On the morning of 5 November the carriers launched twenty-three Avenger torpedo aircraft, twenty-two Dauntless dive-bombers and fifty-two Hellcat fighters from a range of 230 nautical miles. They out-manoeuvred the seventy Japanese fighters sent to meet them, attacked through heavy AA fire and damaged the cruisers *Maya, Atago, Mogami, Takao, Agano* and *Noshiro*, and in so doing eliminated the danger to the American landing fleet. The photograph below shows, in the foreground, the heavy cruiser *Haguro*, which had already been damaged in the battle off

Empress Augusta Bay, a transport set alight by the American bombers and, in the background, further ships and the port installations of Rabaul in flames. On 11 November the two carriers repeated the attack on Rabaul, this time in concert with a formation dispatched to Rabaul by Admiral Nimitz including the new carriers *Essex, Bunker Hill* and *Independence*, and the Americans inflicted further severe damage. In the course of the following weeks the Japanese aircraft which had been transferred to Rabaul were so seriously decimated by American bombers and the long-range Lightning fighters based at the new airfields that Rabaul was effectively neutralised, and could be circumvented by the Americans without any danger.

Japanese ships under attack at Rabaul.

Marine casualties at Tawara atoll.

At the Trident summit conference in May 1943 it had been decided to route the American attack in the Pacific along the coast of New Guinea, through the Celebes sea and then make a landing on the Chinese coast near Hongkong, with the purpose of establishing air bases on the mainland from which B-29 Superfortress bombers could attack Japan. Admirals King and Nimitz foresaw the threat of the Japanese fleet steaming from Truk and Palau to outflank them, and suggested a second direction of advance through the Marshall islands and the Carolines, which plan gave useful employment to the ships now being complet-

ed in the Americans' major building pro- gramme. However, before the attack on the Marshall islands could be carried out, the Japanese air bases on the Gilbert islands had to be eliminated.

On 20 November 1943 the Americans landed on the Gilbert islands of Tarawa and Makin, covered by Task Force 58 which con- sisted of twelve fast carriers with 685 aircraft on board, eight new battleships, nine cruisers and thirty-nine destroyers. With artillery support from seven modernised old battle- ships and other ships, 18,313 men of the 2nd Marine Division landed on Tarawa in two amphibious groups, and 6,507 men of the 7th

Infantry Division on Makin. In the attack on Betio, the main island of the Tarawa atoll, the amphibious vessels struck coral reefs in the lagoon. The marines then had to wade to the beach through a long expanse of water under continuous Japanese fire, and by the evening the beach was littered with corpses, as shown in the photograph here. It took three days for the Americans to overcome the 4,800 Japanese defenders on the island, although it was only 2,500yds by 500yds in area. The Americans lost 1,009 dead and 2,101 wound- ed, the Japanese 4,654 dead and only 146 captured.

(above) US ships landing supplies on Hollandia.

(left) Japanese destroyer *Tanikaze* under attack.

(top left) Japanese torpedo-plane shot down by USS *Yorktown*

After the severe loss of ships due to the American carrier raids against Rabaul, the Japanese were unable to put their fleet into action, and were forced to restrict themselves to submarine operations, one of which sank the escort carrier *Liscome Bay*, and attacks by land-based aircraft. These aircraft – like the Jill torpedo aircraft in the photograph opposite in the process of being shot down by the AA guns of the new carrier *Yorktown* – were seldom able to break through the protective cordon and reach the

US ships.

Armed with the experience of the Gilbert operation, the American 5th Fleet with its two amphibious groups and the carriers of the Fast Carrier Task Force 58 attacked the main Japanese base in the Marshall islands, the Kwajalein atoll, on 31 January 1944. A third formation captured the Majuro atoll without having to fire a weapon. After two days of bombardments by the 700 carrier aircraft and ships' artillery the landings were successfully carried out with much smaller losses than on previous occasions. Of the 41,446 landed troops 372 fell and 1,582 were wounded. Of the 8,675 defenders only 265 were taken prisoner, and most of them were Korean building workers. The landing on Eniwetok atoll, which took place in the peri-

od 17 to 22 February, passed off even more efficiently. In an effort to eliminate any chance of a counter-attack from the Japanese base of Truk, Task Force 58 attacked the islands on 17 and 18 February en masse, but only found stragglers to attack, such as the destroyer *Tanikaze* shown in the photograph opposite, since by this time the Japanese had escaped by transferring their fleet to Palau. The Americans sank five auxiliary ships, six tankers and seventeen freighters amounting to around 200,000 tons. In the meantime MacArthur, supported by Task Force 58, made a great leap from New Guinea westward to Hollandia, and in so doing isolated the Japanese 18th Army. The photograph here shows American landing ships unloading supplies on the jungle beach of Hollandia.

By the spring of 1944 the US Pacific Fleet had received a considerable number of newly completed ships to add to the Fast Carrier Task Force as well as the amphibious attack groups, and these new vessels added considerable weight to the American offensive in the central Pacific area. The Majuro atoll, which the Americans occupied in November 1943, proved to be an excellent anchorage for the 5th Fleet and its logistical units, since it had a very large lagoon. In the picture above three new Cleveland-class light cruisers and three new aircraft carriers lie at anchor in the broad reaches of the lagoon.

Even so, right up to the autumn of 1944 arguments raged between the Chiefs of Staff in Washington and Admiral Nimitz on the one hand and General MacArthur on the other. The point at dispute was the priority of the direction of advance – the central Pacific route versus the southern route. General MacArthur wanted to liberate the Philippines on his southern route before carrying out a landing on the Chinese mainland, so that preparations could be made to attack Japan from the air and, if necessary, carry

US cruisers and carriers at Majuro atoll, November 1943.

out landings there subsequently. Admiral Nimitz considered that the shorter route to the Philippine island of Luzon or even Formosa would be the better choice. In any case he claimed that conquering the Mariana Islands beforehand would permit B-29 attacks on Japan to be carried out much earlier. Eventually, the decision was made to attack the Marianas in mid-June.

It was planned that Japanese positions in the rearward regions such as Truk should be suppressed from the air before the Marianas were occupied. On or after 15 September 1944 landings would be carried out on Palau, Yap and Morotai, on 15 November on Mindanao, on 20 December on Leyte and in late February 1945 on Luzon or Formosa.

In March 1944 Admiral Koga had moved the Japanese defence line back to the Kurils, the Marianas and the western part of New Guinea, and intended to assemble all his forces at this line and force the US Pacific Fleet into battle. In preparation for this he moved his fleet away from the area dominated by the US carriers and into the Moluccas region, just before a US carrier raid against Palau on 30 and 31 March. Koga's flying boat disappeared en route to Mindanao, and he was presumed dead. He was succeeded by Admiral Toyoda.

The first stage of the operation was to construct airfields on Hollandia. On 17 May MacArthur used the 7th Fleet, now under his command, to land a regiment on Wakde, and on 27 May he landed the remainder of the 41st Division on Biak. These islands off the coast gave the Americans air superiority extending to the west of New Guinea. Admiral Toyoda made two attempts to relieve Biak and prevent the landing on the island. The first attempt employed light forces in a night-time operation, which was repulsed by an Australian-American task force, while the second, utilising the battleships *Yamato* and *Musashi* was broken off when the Americans landed on the Mariana island of Saipan on 15 June. Several days of bombardment by the aircraft of fifteen carriers of Task Force 58 and fourteen escort carriers of the amphibious groups, together with the heavy artillery of the battleships and cruisers, preceded the landing of the first waves of the 2nd and 4th Marine Divisions on Saipan. The photograph below shows the battleship *New Mexico* off Saipan, firing a salvo from its 15in triple turret, with her sistership the *Idaho* in the background. By the evening of the first day about 20,000 men had been landed from the 396 amphibious ships. In spite of determined counter-attacks, the bridgehead in the south of the islands was secured on 21 June.

Battleship USS *New Mexico* bombarding Saipan; USS *Idaho* in background.

Since the possession of the Marianas opened up to the Americans the possibility of attacking the Japanese mainland with long-range bombers, the Japanese threw every effort into an attempt to frustrate the American landing on Saipan. Thus it was that 19 June 1944 saw the battle of the Philippine Sea.

The Japanese fleet consisted of nine aircraft carriers, five battleships, thirteen cruisers and twenty-eight destroyers, and the Japanese intention was to launch their 430 carrier aircraft for an attack on the US carrier fleet before their own ships were within range of the American aircraft. At the same time their land-based aircraft, stationed on the Mariana islands of Tinian, Guam and Rota which were still under Japanese occupation, were to attack the landing fleet. The aircraft were then to be re-fuelled and re-armed on the island airfields and carry out a second attack against the US fleet on the return flight to the carriers. Operating on information from radio intelligence, American submarines reported the approach of the Japanese battle formations at an early stage, so that Task Force 58 under Admiral

(top left) US fighter landing, June 1944.

(bottom left) Japanese carrier *Zuikaku* evading bombs.

(above) US troops board landing ship for attack on Angaur.

Mitscher, consisting of fifteen carriers, seven battleships, twenty-one cruisers and sixty-seven destroyers, was able to intercept them in good time. Two hundred and seventy-two of the approaching Japanese carrier aircraft were shot down by American fighters after they had been detected by radar, and none of the American ships suffered serious damage. The Americans referred to the operation as 'a turkey shoot', and one of their aircraft is shown in the picture at top left landing back on the carrier after a mission. The American submarines *Albacore* and *Cavalla* had torpe-

doed the two carriers *Taiho* and *Shokaku* on the morning of 19 June 1944. Major fuel fires broke out, and both ships sank that afternoon. When Admiral Ozawa, the Commander of the Japanese formations, initiated a withdrawal after the disastrous Japanese losses in carriers and aircraft, Mitscher took up the pursuit and on the afternoon of 20 June launched his aircraft for a counter-strike. Although his carriers had reduced the distance, they were still right at the limit of his aircraft's range. The Japanese were taken by surprise as dusk fell and their aircraft were being re-fuelled. The carrier *Hiyo* and two tankers were sunk and the carriers *Zuikaku*, shown in the picture on the left trying to escape the falling bombs, *Junyo*, *Ryuho* and *Chiyoda* and three other ships were damaged. Of the 216 American aircraft which took off, twenty were shot down, and eighty

failed to reach their carriers in the darkness due to lack of petrol, although US submarines only failed to pick up thirty-eight men of the aircraft crews. In the battle of the Philippines Sea the Japanese lost, in addition to three aircraft carriers, approximately 450 aircraft, against the Americans 129. For Japan the battle had been a catastrophe.

The fighting on Saipan dragged on until 9 July. Of the 67,451 Americans who had landed, 3,426 were killed and 13,099 were wounded, while 23,811 of the Japanese defenders were killed and 1,780 taken prisoner. On 21 July 1944 the Americans landed on Guam, and on 24 July on Tinian, whose defenders were overcome on 2 August.

The picture at the top was taken in September, and shows US soldiers climbing aboard a landing ship prior to the attack on the Palau island of Angaur.

(above) Landing ships at Leyte, September 1944.

(left) Japanese survivor rescued by *PT 321*.

On 15 September 1944 the Americans landed on the Moluccan island of Morotai. Morotai and the Palau islands, which were occupied at the same time, were important air bases in the plan to re-capture the Philippines. The Americans now undertook repeated heavy air attacks against Japanese airfields and port installations on Formosa and the Philippines, destroying hundreds of Japanese aircraft.

In September the air attacks carried out by the fast carriers of what was now known as Task Force 38 against the central Philippines showed up an unexpected weakness on the part of the Japanese, and in consequence the Americans called off the landing on the southern Philippines island of Mindanao which had been planned for December. Instead of this, four divisions were landed further north on Leyte on 20 October 1944. The top picture here shows a number of landing ships, with *LSM 311* in the foreground, carrying sections of the 1st Cavalry Division towards the beach at the north of the bridgehead. In the picture on the left a shipwrecked Japanese is pulled from the water by crew members of the US fast boat *PT 321*, which had run through into the Surigao Strait between Leyte and Mindanao. The photograph below shows a wounded American being carried onto a landing boat by fellow soldiers.

The Japanese 16th Division defending Leyte withdrew into the hilly hinterland, still fighting a rearguard action, while the Japanese Sho-Go operation continued. This was intended to be a crucial action in which the US fleet would be defeated and the American landing on Leyte would be stopped. The Japanese planned to divert the American carrier groups away from the landing area to the east of Leyte by bringing their surviving four carriers, two battleships and three cruisers down from the North. In so doing they hoped to liberate their own battle fleet consisting of seven battleships and twelve heavy cruisers, approaching the

Philippines from the west in two groups, so that they could penetrate through the Sibuyan Sea and the straits of San Bernardino and Surigao, and carry out a pincer attack on the US landing fleet in the Gulf of Leyte, which by then would only be weakly defended. The Japanese attack was to be supported by seventeen submarines together with army and navy aircraft, while transports were to bring reinforcements from four divisions into the Ormoc bay on the Western side of Leyte by sea.

On the American side General MacArthur had command of the landing forces and the supporting 7th Fleet, which comprised eighteen escort carriers, six old battleships and nine cruisers. Admiral Nimitz retained command of Admiral Halsey's 3rd Fleet, consisting of eight large fleet carriers, eight light carriers, six battleships and fifteen cruisers. These ships were intended to cover the landing and at the same time attack and destroy the Japanese fleet if the oppor-

tunity arose.

The two enemy fleets approached each other, and in the period 23 to 26 October 1944 engaged in the battle of Leyte, which was made up of four battles held in the Sibuyan Sea, the Surigao strait, off Samar and near Cape Engaño. It involved thirty-eight aircraft carriers, twenty-one battleships, forty-three cruisers, 146 destroyers and numerous other ships, approximately 1,500 aircraft and 183,000 men, and as such represents the greatest naval battle of all time.

On 23 October the submarines *Darter* and *Dace* sighted the Japanese formation approaching from the west off the north-west coast of Palawan, and torpedoed the cruisers *Atago* and *Maya*, which sank, and the *Takao*, which was forced to turn back.

Wounded US soldier being carried back to landing craft.

Survivors from the burning carrier USS *Princeton* awaiting rescue.

The sixteen American aircraft carriers of Task Force 38 were divided into four groups, of which three were stationed to the east of the Philippine islands of Samar and Luzon in order to cover the landing on Leyte and suppress the Japanese airfields, while the fourth group re-fuelled from the supply fleet further east. When the submarines reported the approach of the Japanese fleet on 23 October, the carriers launched spotter aircraft heading west.

On the morning of the 24th they sighted the Japanese main force steaming from the west, at the southern tip of Mindoro in the entrance to the Sibuyan Sea. This was the most powerful group: that of Admiral Kurita with five battleships, nine cruisers and fifteen destroyers. Further south they picked up another formation in the Sulu Sea, with two battleships, one cruiser and four destroyers. Admiral Halsey ordered an immediate attack with all available forces and recalled the fourth carrier group from the supply area.

In the meantime the Japanese had launched three waves of between fifty and sixty aircraft to attack the US carriers. They were intercepted by American fighters, but one broke though and hit the carrier *Princeton* with a 250kg bomb. Severe fires and explosions occurred which caused further losses on those ships which came to the *Princeton*'s aid, and the carrier subsequently had to be abandoned. The photograph above shows survivors on rafts awaiting their rescue by one of the escort ships.

Japanese battleships *Musashi (top)* and *Yamashiro (bottom)* under air attack.

Admiral Kurita's battle formation had now reached the Sibuyan Sea, and at this stage the aircraft of two of the American carrier groups attacked his ships in a series of waves. The Japanese AA fire was initially intense but it soon diminished, and the fighter protection from Luzon which had been assigned to them failed to appear, and in consequence only eighteen of the 259 American machines on the attack were shot down. The Americans most important success was that they hit one of the two Japanese super-battleships, the *Musashi*, with nineteen aerial torpedoes and seventeen bombs, and the ship sank the same evening. The picture at top right shows the *Musashi* in the midst of a storm of bombs, and already severely damaged. The cruiser *Myoko* was also hit and was forced to turn back. Kurita decided to take his ships off to the west for a while, to await the success of Japanese aircraft attacks on the US carriers. The Japanese battle group with the old battleships *Yamashiro* (shown in the photograph at bottom right) and *Fuso* was approaching through the Sulu Sea when she was also attacked by the Americans, although no serious damage was done. The change of course by Kurita's formation and the exaggerated reports of success by the American pilots caused Halsey to assume that the danger from the west had been eliminated. He therefore took his three fast carrier groups to the north in order to attack the Japanese carrier formation detected on the afternoon of 24 October. In so doing he allowed himself to be drawn away from Leyte.

On the night of 25 October the southern Japanese battle group pressed in from the Sulu Sea to the Southern coast of Leyte. At the northern outlet of the Surigao Strait the Japanese encountered the six battleships of the 7th US Fleet together with several cruisers and destroyers, and the American ships' lethal radar-guided artillery and torpedoes inflicted tremendous damage. The battleships *Yamashiro* and *Fuso* were sunk, and the remainder of the formation was forced to retreat.

Halsey's change of course towards the north opened up the way for Kurita to pass through the unguarded San Bernardino Strait after turning back once more. On the morning of 25 October his formation attacked one of the US escort carrier groups off the east coast of Samar. The escort carri-

Kamikaze attack on USS *Intrepid*.

ers were taken by surprise, and attempted to launch their aircraft. In visibility reduced by the smoke of the accompanying escort vessels, they also attempted to escape from the Japanese threat. Kurita's ships sank the escort carrier *Gambier Bay* and three American destroyers. Eleven Kamikaze pilots took part in this action – the first to do

so. They dived their bomb-laden aircraft directly onto the American ships, sacrificing their lives at the same time. In the picture at the top of the facing page very young Japanese pilots report for take-off and reconcile themselves to imminent death. In the picture at the bottom of the page the American carrier *St Lo* explodes after being struck by a suicide aircraft, and six others were more or less severely damaged in the

same way in the battle of Samar. The air attacks by the US escort carrier aircraft and the fear of the arrival of Halsey's carrier fleet caused Kurita to break off the attack before he could offer a threat to the American landing fleet off Leyte, to which he had approached worryingly close. Halsey was recalled, but he arrived too late to intercept Kurita before he reached the San Bernardino Strait.

At the time the battle off Samar was raging, on the morning of 25 October, 527 aircraft from Halsey's carrier groups attacked and sank the Japanese aircraft carriers *Chitose*, *Zuikaku*, *Zuiho* and *Chiyoda* off Cape Engano to the north-east of the Philippine island of Luzon. On 25 and 26 October more retreating Japanese ships were sunk by aircraft.

The battle of Leyte cost the Japanese their last four serviceable carriers, three battleships, ten cruisers and around 10,000 dead, while the Americans lost three smaller carriers and about 1,500 men. The Japanese fleet no longer constituted an instrument of battle which had to be taken seriously.

From this time on the Kamikaze pilots represented a constant threat to the American ships. On 25 November 1944 one of them dived onto the carrier *Intrepid* operating off Luzon and caused severe damage. The photograph on the left records the instant before the impact. The air is filled with exploding AA shells from the carrier's guns.

(right) Kamikaze pilots.

(below) US carrier *St Lo* hit by suicide plane.

USS *Saratoga* burning after repeated kamikaze hits.

At the end of 1944 discussions were held amongst the American chiefs of staff on the location for the next American landings: either the Philippine island of Luzon or Formosa and China. MacArthur's view prevailed: air bases were captured on Mindoro to the south of Manila on 15 December 1944, and on 9 January 1945 four divisions of the 6th Army landed in the Lingayen Gulf on the western coast of Luzon.

In the course of the next few months MacArthur carried out numerous landings in the Philippines and Borneo using the 7th Fleet which he commanded, while the Pacific fleet turned its attention to Japan: in November B-29 aircraft flew the first bomb and fire bomb attacks against Japanese cities from their bases on the Marianas. On the long return flight bombers damaged by AA or Japanese fighters often had to carry out emergency ditchings, and this made it essential to obtain a base for escort fighters and emergency landings at the half-way point. The volcanic island of Iwo Jima with its three airfields was the ideal location for this, and a landing was planned for 19 February. Task Force 58 laid the preparations for this operation with air attacks and then carried out raids against Japan to ward off counter-attacks by Japanese aircraft and – above all – Kamikazes.

On the afternoon of 21 February 1945 the veteran aircraft carrier *Saratoga* was operating just such a mission, providing fighter protection to the landing fleet, when within the space of three minutes the ship was hit by five Kamikazes and by a further one some time later, and the damage was so grievous that she was out of service for three months. The picture on the left shows teams on the deck of the *Saratoga* dousing burning, battle-ready aircraft which had been set on fire by the Kamikazes. Thirty-six aircraft were burned out or thrown overboard, and six more had to ditch in the sea. One hundred and twenty-three men were killed and 192 wounded. During these operations the most serious damage of all was inflicted on the *Franklin*: on 19 March 1945 during an attack on Japanese fleet bases in the Inland Sea the ship was hit by two bombs while her aircraft were being launched. Seven hundred and

twenty-four members of the crew were killed in the attack and 265 were wounded, but the ship was brought back home.

During the landing by the 4th and 5th American Marine Divisions on the 2.5 km wide south-east beach of Iwo Jima on 19 February 1945, the marines ran into devastating flanking fire from Japanese gun batteries built into the volcanic cone of Mount Suribachi. The Japanese pinned them down on the terraced volcanic ash beach. By the end of the first day 2,420 men lay dead, and the marines had only made it through to the opposite coast at the narrowest point of the island. The picture below shows fallen marines in a bomb crater on the terraced beach, with landing ships and transports in the background. On 23 February Mount Suribachi was captured, but in the central mountainous part of the island the Japanese defenders under General Kuribayashi put up

a determined and bitter resistance.

The 3rd Marine Division, which had been held in reserve, eventually had to be landed on 24 February, and one week later the greater part of the island was in American hands, but remnants of the Japanese force held out until 26 March and then streamed out of their bunkers in a suicide attack. The battle for Iwo Jima cost the Americans 6,821 dead and 19,189 wounded, the Japanese 21,304 dead. Only 212 Japanese survivors, most of them wounded, were taken prisoner.

The airfields on the island were immediately expanded by the Americans, and on 7 April P-51 fighters took off from the new base to provide fighter protection for B-29 bombers flying to Japan. By the end of the war 2,251 B-29s with 24,761 crewmen had made emergency landings on Iwo Jima.

US marines killed on Iwo Jima.

The destruction of Japanese merchant shipping grew steadily to catastrophic proportions, and a major part in this was played by Ultra decrypts: in early 1943 the Allies succeeded in breaking the so-called Japanese Maru code, a superenciphered 4-letter code which was used to give course directions to Japanese merchant ships, whose names ended in the suffix 'Maru'. Although the American submarines were few in number in comparison with the size of the Pacific ocean, this information allowed the controllers to direct them very accurately to positions where the Japanese transports had to pass. In November 1943 the Japanese, who had given little attention to protecting sea transport until this time, adopted the convoy system generally for their shipping. The Americans responded by employing their submarines in teams of three, and sought out tankers, escorts and large transports as special targets for their 'wolf-pack' attacks.

During the night of 11/12 September 1944 a team of three submarines attacked a Japanese convoy consisting of nine ships and seven escorts. The submarine *Growler* sank two escorts, while the other two – *Sealion* and *Pampanito* – sent two transports and two tankers to the bottom. Of these transports the *Rakuyo Maru* and *Kachidoki Maru* were carrying 1,350 and 750 British and Australian prisoners respectively. The Japanese rescued their own survivors but left the allied prisoners to their fate in the water. It was not until three days later that the *Pampanito* discovered a raft carrying survivors, and she called the *Sealion* to come to her assistance. The two boats picked up 121 oil-soaked and exhausted men, as shown in the photograph above, taken from the *Sealion*, and another submarine team rescued a further thirty men.

On 26 March 1945 the greatest amphibious attack of the Pacific war began –

(above) US prisoners from sunken Japanese transports rescued by US submarine *Sealion*.

(top right) Rocket bombardment of Tokashiki Jima.

(bottom left) 'Amtracks' from *LST 782*.

Operation Iceberg against Okinawa – with the landing of the American 77th Division on the offshore group of islands called Kerama Retto. The picture at top right shows the medium landing ships *LSM(R) 196*, *190* and *199* firing rocket salvoes at Japanese positions on Tokashiki Jima. The landing on Okinawa itself began on 1 April. In the picture on the right two 'Amtrack' amphibious vehicles are seen leaving the bow ramp of *LST 782* on 4 April, with small landing craft still lashed to the hull side.

LCTs landing supplies on Okinawa.

By October 1944 the American Chiefs of Staff had abandoned thoughts of a landing on Formosa or the Chinese mainland, and instead planned to capture Okinawa prior to landings in Japan. This would gain them airfields for land-based aircraft in the vicinity of the main Japanese islands.

Preparatory attacks lasting weeks were made against Japanese bases in Kyushu, the most southerly main Japanese island, by carrier aircraft and B-29 bombers based on the Marianas. Attacks were also carried out on the Riukiu islands, including heavy bombardments by ships' artillery, before the 6th and 1st Marine Divisions and the 7th and 96th Army Divisions landed alongside each other on the south-west of Okinawa. The American 'Joint Expeditionary Force' assembled for this operation consisted of a total of 1,213 ships. Amongst them were fourteen escort carriers carrying 564 aircraft, ten old battleships, thirteen cruisers and twenty-three destroyers to provide artillery support. The majority of the vessels were landing ships and landing craft, some of which can be seen in the picture above, showing LCTs on the beach of Okinawa unloading goods for a supply base, with numerous landing ships and larger transports in the background. Task Force 58, which also participated, consisted of fifteen carriers, eight battleships, fifteen cruisers and forty-eight destroyers, and carried a total of 919 shipborne aircraft. There was also one British task group on hand, consisting of four carriers, two battleships, four cruisers, twelve destroyers and 244 aircraft. Initial Japanese resistance was slight, and the two main airfields were captured on the very first day. The Japanese planned to keep the 77,000 men of her 32nd Army in readiness in protected positions, concentrated in the southern part of Okinawa, ready to throw the landed forces back into the sea in a counter-attack once her fleet and the Kamikaze pilots had completed a successful attack on the American landing fleet. In consequence the US marines were soon able to occupy the Northern part of the island with little opposition, while the XXIV Corps came up against the Japanese mountain positions and hardly made any progress.

On the afternoon of 6 April 1945 the Japanese began their counter-attack against the US fleet off Okinawa. From the Inland Sea the battleship *Yamato*, the cruiser *Yahagi* and eight destroyers put to sea, and from Kyushu and Formosa 344 bombers and 355 Kamikaze aircraft took off to attack the American landing fleet, which was surrounded by early warning 'radar picket' ships, most of them destroyers. Although American fighters and AA guns shot down many of the Japanese aircraft, nine American destroyers and eight other ships were hit so hard that they either sank or were eliminated from the rest of the war. Six further ships, amongst them the carrier *Hancock*, were damaged. Four hundred and eighty-four American sailors died and 582 were wounded. By this time an American submarine had picked up the *Yamato* group outside the Bungo Strait.

On the morning of 7 April the spotters of Task Force 58 reported the *Yamato* forma-tion, which was striking out into the East China Sea ready to attack. Admiral Mitscher ordered 280 aircraft to take off from the two task groups which were within range. Shortly after midday they attacked the Japanese ships in four waves, hitting the *Yamato* with ten torpedoes and five bombs, with the result that the ship sank after two hours. The *Yahagi* also sank after being struck by twelve bombs and seven torpedoes, and four Japanese destroyers met the same fate. Three thousand six hundred and sixty-five Japanese seamen went down with their ships, 209 mostly wounded survivors were rescued. The Americans lost ten aircraft and twelve men. Although the Japanese plan had failed, the defenders on Okinawa carried on their rearguard action and continued to fly Kamikaze attacks.

It was not until 21 June 1945 that the Japanese defenders of Okinawa were finally overcome. Around 131,000 soldiers and inhabitants of the island lost their lives in the struggle, while only 7,401 men were taken prisoner. On the American side the losses were also high: the Army and Marine Corps counted 7,213 dead, amongst them the com-mander of the 10th Army, General Buckner, and 31,081 wounded. The destruction amongst the American fleet was substantial: thirty-six ships were sunk, twenty-six of them as a result of Kamikaze attacks, and 368 ships suffered more or less severe dam-age, of which 164 were due to the Japanese suicide pilots. Four thousand nine hundred and seven Americans had been killed on the ships, and 4824 wounded. The picture below shows casualties from a carrier hit by a Kamikaze being committed to the sea by their fellows. These losses were a bad omen for the great landings in Japan, planned for November 1945 and March 1946.

US sailors killed by kamikaze attack buried at sea.

Admiral Mitscher's flagship was the aircraft carrier *Bunker Hill*, and the photograph on the left shows the ship in flames on 11 May 1945 after receiving two Kamikaze aircraft strikes near Okinawa. Three hundred and ninety-six men died in the attacks, and 264 were wounded. The ship was brought home but stayed out of commission for the rest of

(left) USS *Bunker Hill* hit by two kamikaze attacks.

(below) Sinking of the Japanese battleship *Yamato*.

(bottom) *William D Porter* sinking.

the war. The picture immediately below was taken from an attacking American dive bomber, and shows two of the aircraft's bombs exploding on the Japanese battleship *Yamato* (see page 185). The bottom picture shows one of the last American losses of the war: on 10 June the 'picket' destroyer *William D Porter* suffered a near-miss by a Kamikaze pilot, but the aircraft's bomb exploded under water, and sixty-two men died from shock injuries. The ship sank, but all of the surviving crew was rescued by the minesweeper *YMS 122* and four landing craft.

After an uninterrupted period of active service at sea lasting more than three months – the duration of the Okinawa operation – with their only source of supply being tanker formations, Task Force 38 resumed its attacks on Japan on 10 July 1945, after just a brief pause. Tokyo was the target on the 10th, Hokkaido on the 14th and 15th, Tokyo again on the 18 and the Inland Sea bases on 24th, 25th and 28 July. The photograph above shows the Japanese heavy cruiser *Tone* off Kure on 24 July, enveloped in the smoke of American bombs. Renewed attacks followed on 30 July against Tokyo-Nagoya, against Hokkaido and North Honshu on 9th and 10th and on Tokyo again on 13th and 15 August.

American battleships and cruisers pounded the coast.

During these operations any Japanese warships still afloat were destroyed or sunk, the Kamikaze pilots' airfields were bombarded and land installations placed under artillery fire.

On 8 August 1945, in accordance with the

north-eastern coast of Korea, behind the Japanese front. The photograph below shows Soviet naval infantrymen en route to a landing in Seishin on 14 August. At the same time units of the Soviet North Pacific Flotilla carried out amphibious operations with landing ships on the Japanese Kuril islands using landing ships, as shown in the photograph at the bottom of the page. The islands were occupied by 2 September.

(left) Japanese heavy cruiser *Tone* under air attack off Kure.

(below) Soviet troops en route to the Kurile islands.

(bottom) Soviets landing on the Kurile islands.

conditions agreed at the Potsdam Conference held on July 1945 and signed by the victorious powers after the end of the war in Europe, the Soviet Union declared war on Japan. While the Soviet 25th Army advanced towards Korea, the Soviet Pacific Fleet completed a series of landings in ports on the

Over the last few decades there has been much discussion about the likelihood of Japan surrendering if the two atom bombs had not been dropped on Hiroshima and Nagasaki. There can be no question that Japan had no chance of producing a favourable end to the war after late July 1945. Her losses in merchant shipping, primarily due to the action of the American submarines, and the absolute naval superiority of the Allies outside the immediate Japanese coastal region had cut off Japan from its supplies of raw materials and oil, without which its industry could produce nothing. In any case, Japanese industry was under constantly increasing bombard-

ment by the B-29 bombers of the 20th Air Force based on the Marianas, and by Allied carrier aircraft, against which they could offer virtually no defence.

The more judicious bodies in Japan recognised this fact, and sought through Soviet mediation to find a course of action which at least might leave the position of the Emperor untouched. However, these efforts encountered the determined resistance of the army and its commanders, whose core, stationed in Japan, Korea and Manchuria, was still far from defeated. The Fleet Chief also opposed any softening of the Japanese stance, preferring to continue the fight for

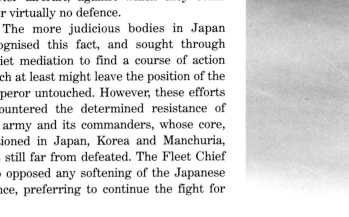

(right) USS *Missouri* in Sagami Bay, with Mount Fuji behind.

(below) Signing of Japanese surrender aboard USS Missouri.

the honour of Japan. Since the Soviets rejected the discreet advances on the part of the Japanese, the decision was left in the air. The American government and Chiefs of Staff, mindful of their bitter experiences on Okinawa, were faced with the decision whether to continue the war with the devastating incendiary bomb attacks on Japanese cities and eventually the inevitable heavy losses on both sides which would be incurred in the planned attack landings, or to bring about a rapid conclusion with one or two massive blows with the new, still untested weapon.

On 16 July the test detonation of the atom bomb showed that the device could be expected to function correctly, and President Truman then decided to inflict the weapon on Japan if that country did not immediately agree to the conditions of the Potsdam

Declaration of 26 July. This demanded her unconditional surrender, but did not mention the position of the Emperor directly. Violent arguments occurred at the very highest level of the Japanese Command, but no clear decision was taken. On 2 August, when no unambiguous answer had been received, President Truman, on his return journey from Potsdam on board the cruiser *Augusta*, gave the order to drop the atomic bomb. During the night of 6 August 1945 the B-29 'Enola Gay' took off from the Mariana island of Tinian and dropped the atom bomb on the city of Hiroshima. Including those who died as a consequence of radioactive fall-out, the attack cost the lives of a quarter of a million people.

Now events followed their own momentum. On the morning of 9 August, the Japanese Lord Keeper of the Privy Seal,

Marquis Kido, called a meeting of the 'Council for the conduct of the war' at the direction of the Emperor. This meeting was due to discuss the ramifications of the bomb on Hiroshima and the Soviet declaration of war, but news then arrived that a second atom bomb had been dropped on Nagasaki. After seven hours of fruitless discussion the Emperor himself was asked for his decision. He ordered that the Potsdam Declaration should be accepted, and that Japan should therefore surrender.

After an exchange of notes via Switzerland the armistice came into force on 15 August, after the Emperor himself had make his decision known in a radio announcement – itself an entirely unprecedented procedure.

On 28 August the American 2nd Air Landing Division landed at the Atsugi air-

field near Tokyo, and a Marine landing division landed at Yokosuka. On the same day the flagship of the 3rd US Fleet, the battleship *Missouri*, entered Sagami Bay off Tokyo, followed by hundreds of American and Commonwealth ships. The photograph above shows the *Missouri* at anchor with the holy Mount Fuji behind her. The photograph on the left shows the signing of the Japanese surrender in front of General MacArthur on 2nd September 1945 on board the *Missouri*.

Index

The index includes the names of all the ships and individuals mentioned in the text. Ships' names are printed in italics. Where a name is included more than once, it applies to different ships. Aircraft types, operations, dockyards, technical apparatus and certain specialist terms are also included. Individual convoys are grouped together under the entry 'Convoys'.